RESEAR
educati

RESEARCH GUIDE IN
education

John A. R. Wilson
University of California
Santa Barbara

Consulting Editor: Carl Kalvelage

GENERAL LEARNING PRESS
250 James Street
Morristown, New Jersey 07960

Manufactured in the United States of America

Published simultaneously in Canada

Library of Congress Catalog Card Number 76-3307

ISBN 0-382-19048-3

Preface

Many people are concerned about the purported lack of learning among students at all grade levels from kindergarten through college. Some this concern is based on nostalgia for schools as they were in the past, but some is based on a real decline in computational and writing competence. It is my hope that *Research Guide in Education* will give students at least some of the help they may need in the areas of researching and writing.

The guide is divided into three sections. Part I gives a brief overview of education as a discipline. Part II covers the many sources that students can consult in writing an education paper, the kinds of papers required for specific fields, and the problem of picking a topic. Finally, in Part III, the actual writing of a paper is discussed in step-by-step fashion.

Most of the points discussed in the guide are the result of my personal experience with students over the years. I believe that I have some feeling for the kind of help students are likely to need and hope that this feeling is reflected in the pages that follow.

John A. R. Wilson

Acknowledgements

I wish to thank the authors and publishers listed below for the use of materials written and published by them. Formal acknowledgement is provided in the text where the materials appear, and this acknowledgement is keyed to the bibliography.

The National Institute of Education, Department of Health, Education, and Welfare, and the U.S. Government Printing Office, Washington, D.C.

List of ERIC Clearinghouses–Table 1
Document Resumes RIE–Figure 1
Sample Subject Index RIE–Figure 2
Sample Author Index RIE–Figure 3
Sample Institution Index RIE–Figure 4
Main Entry CIJE–Figure 5
Descriptor Groups CIJE
Subject Index CIJE–Figure 6
Author Index CIJE–Figure 7
Journal Contents Index CIJE–Figure 8

Oscar K. Buros and the Gryphon Press for permission to print the table of contents of the *Seventh Mental Measurement Yearbook*.

Carl Kalvelage, Morley Segal, and Peter J. Anderson and General Learning Press for permission to use the material on footnotes and bibliography from *Research Guide for Undergraduates in Political Science*.

The National Society for the Study of Education for permission to use three sample footnotes from Harris, 1968, p. 169; Light and Laufer, 1975, p. 103; and Joyce, 1975, p. 128.

I would like to thank my son, John R. M. Wilson, for having involved me in this project. Most especially I want to thank my wife, Nora, for reading and editing the manuscript before it was sent to the publishers.

Contents

PART I • *The Diversity of Education*
  as a Discipline   **1**

An Overview of Education   **3**

Philosophical Inquiry   **3**
Historical Inquiry   **5**
Sociological Research in Education   **6**
Economics of Education   **6**
Growth and Development   **7**
Educational Psychology   **8**
Tests and Measurements   **9**
Curriculum and Methods   **9**

PART II • *How to Research a Paper*
  in Education   **13**

Selecting, Defining, and Organizing a Topic   **15**

Reading the Literature   **16**
Limiting the Topic   **20**
Organizing the Evidence   **21**

Using the Library   **23**

Dewey Decimal Classification   **24**
Library of Congress Classification   **25**
ERIC-Educational Resources Information Center   **28**

Education Index   **46**
Psychological Abstracts   **48**
Child Development Abstracts and Bibliography   **52**
Sociological Abstracts   **53**
Sociology of Education Abstracts   **54**
Buros Mental Measurement Yearbooks   **55**
Preparing a Bibliography   **58**

Papers in Specific Fields   **59**

Philosophy of Education   **60**
History of Education   **61**
Educational Sociology   **64**
Economics of Education   **68**
Growth and Development   **69**
Educational Psychology   **72**
Measurement and Evaluation   **77**
Counseling and Guidance   **80**
Curriculum and Methods   **81**

PART III • *How to Write a Paper*
in Education   **85**

Content of the Paper   **87**

The Topic   **88**
The Finding   **89**
The Background of the Study   **89**
Your Methods   **89**
Your Findings   **90**
Your Conclusions   **90**
Your Findings' Use in Teaching   **90**

Clarity in Writing   **91**

Say It Concisely and Effectively   **91**
Sharpening Your Writing   **92**

Form of the Paper 96

Typing the Body of the Report 98
Headings 98
Illustrations and Figures 99
Tables 102

Documentation 105

Footnotes 105
What to Footnote 106
Footnote and Bibliography Form 112

Bibliography 126

Index 129

Part I

THE DIVERSITY OF EDUCATION
AS A DISCIPLINE

An Overview of Education

As in such other professions as architecture, medicine, and engineering, education is a name given to professional activities that depend on many subspecialties. Many branches of education will require that you write research papers, but the kind of paper required will vary depending on the area that you are studying. All of these fields require that you review what has already been learned before you design an experiment or produce a finding of your own. This need for background is just as important in experimental educational psychology as it is in the history of education. It may help you to have an overview of the more important areas in which you may need to write papers. Some of the specific research procedures associated with these different areas will be discussed later in the book; this overview is designed only to show you the broad outlines of the various subspecialties in the profession of education.

PHILOSOPHICAL INQUIRY

The major concern of philosophical studies in education is to determine the answers to such questions as: What should be taught? Why should there be public education? Who should pay for education? As you approach the philosophy of education for the first time, you are likely to assume that answers to the preceding questions are obvious. There have always been schools and everybody goes. Of course, as you learn more, you recognize your assumption to be false except as it applies to the recent past and to the industrialized world. Even in the present day United States, philosophical questions are again becoming serious and troublesome problems for educators.

Questions as to whether prekindergarten classes should be established and state supported hinge on basic assumptions about the nature of children. Is there a maturational sequence that makes certain kinds of instruction useless or damaging if provided too early in life? This point of view can be extrapolated from the work of Piaget. Is the environment the determiner of all learning as some followers of B. F. Skinner would hold? What rights do parents have compared to the needs of the society at large? In this context Uri Bronfenbrenner has suggested that children from third generation welfare families should be removed from the home and brought up in communal nurseries such as those operated by the kibbutzim in Israel or by the kindergartens in the U.S.S.R.

Other active and live issues include whether compulsory education is desirable and if so up until what age? 11? 14? 16? 18? 25? On what basis do you make a decision? Should state money be used to support private/parochial schools, or does this violate the separation of church and state? Does the fact that the Constitution mandates the separation of church and state mean that the question of state support for nonpublic education is not subject to debate? Should the schools be open all year round? Should children and young people be grouped by ability? Does this kind of grouping deprive less able students of the stimulus of the more able? Does heterogeneous grouping hold back the abler students for the supposed benefit of the less able? On what basis can decisions on this topic be made? Are the same rules valid for colleges and universities as for elementary and high schools? Is heterogeneous admission desirable for a medical school? Is indoctrination to a point of view a defensible goal of education? Should this decision on indoctrination include support for the Constitution of the United States? Communism? Capitalism? The use of drugs? Environmental protection? Going to college?

As you write your own papers on the philosophy of education, you should learn that the answers to these complex questions are difficult and that consistency in applying a principle can lead to uncomfortable decisions. Obviously, you are going to have to behave as though you have a philosophical system even though that system may, on analysis, turn out to be a very inconsistent and chaotic one. Scholarly research on your part, however, will help you to decide what you believe and why you believe it.

HISTORICAL INQUIRY

All research in education involves a substantial element of historical study. Many of the same problems have been coming up for three thousand years or more. Many of the proposed solutions are equally old even when they are paraded as brand new ideas. It helps to know that Quintilian objected two thousand years ago to the idea that "boys should not be taught to read till they are seven years old." He also said, "I am not satisfied with teaching small children the names and order of letters before their shapes." These are still actively debated theories.

   Even in the most experimental research there is a background that needs to be studied. Usually many researchers have contributed to the basic knowledge available, and many of the findings are in conflict with each other. You must learn to locate the sources and to evaluate their authority. This validation of sources is easy to write down but very difficult to apply, especially for a beginner in the field. In any particular study you will also need to evaluate the relevance, meaning, and dependability of the data. The way in which the findings follow from the research design, and the logical tightness of the relation between the findings and their interpretation constitute an internal criterion that will be easier for you to use when you have made a number of analyses. Even for historians with years of experience, there are sharp disagreements about the validity and utility of the material studied. A most important part of your historical review will be getting the ideas down in a clear and logical manner so that your sequence of presentation reveals the relationships that have become clear to you.

SOCIOLOGICAL RESEARCH IN EDUCATION

The effect society has on the learning of students and groups of students has become an important area of study. As a teacher you will be working in a small society created by the school itself. Almost all of your work will be with groups of individuals, since few teachers enjoy the luxury of working with one pupil at a time. As you learn the nature of group processes, particularly as they apply in the school, you should be able to capitalize on the strengths and minimize the weaknesses of social forces. In your research for your papers you will develop an understanding of the meaning of peer pressure and the way peer expectations are able to facilitate or block what you are trying to accomplish. Many of you will work in inner cities, where the social dynamics are not as supportive of the school as they are in the suburbs. Ways to counter the negative effect of this social force have not yet become part of the general wisdom of teachers and, as a consequence, many of the children from inner city schools do badly in all of the measurable criteria of successful school performance. Many, if not most, of these failures occur in spite of the fact that the children possess adequate intelligence to do the work required.

Many of the skills needed for research in the sociology of education are similar to those required in historical and philosophical research, but in addition you must learn to design experiments that test hypotheses about how to divert social forces to benefit students' school work. Success in this area of research can mean that you will have a more satisfying professional life than would be the case if you failed to master the nature of the problems and ways of circumventing them.

ECONOMICS OF EDUCATION

As undergraduates not many of you will become involved in the economics of education except as participants. Very few of you will be asked to write papers in this area although most of you will be concerned with economic decisions that trade off class-size increases against teacher salaries. Instead of doubling every five years as it did in the late 1960s, the school population is declining, and the economic forces that result from this change will have a very intimate and personal effect on you even though you may not have studied the topic formally.

In your work on the history, philosophy, sociology, and economics of education, the emphasis will be on library research. For other aspects of education you will need to use experimental and observational techniques with students in addition to working in the library to discover what is already known about the particular facet of schooling that concerns you at the moment.

GROWTH AND DEVELOPMENT

Much of the research in growth and development is descriptive rather than experimental; that is, people have observed and described the ways in which children behave at different ages. The work of Piaget, Gesell, and Nancy Bayley, among many others, details the changes that take place in the same children over periods of many years. Burton L. White of Harvard University has progressed from an eight-year longitudinal study of the events that occur during development to an experimental design that will test the influence of many variables on those events. There are other experimental designs being used to test hypotheses about causes of differences in developmental patterns. All of these studies require several years before they yield results. Obviously you cannot take a comparable amount of time to turn in your paper to your professor; but no matter what the topic of your paper, watching children will usually make your understanding more concrete. There is a real difference between reading about three-year-olds at play and actually watching them playing. It helps your understanding if there is more than one child to observe, but even watching a single child can make your paper much more vital. In addition, when you are teaching, you will remember the knowledge from observation more vividly than that gathered in the library.

EDUCATIONAL PSYCHOLOGY

Child growth and development is often considered part of educational psychology as is work on tests and measurements. In this chapter, however, we will look at them as separate topics, and in this section the emphasis will be on learning. As a teacher you will be vitally concerned that learning take place, and you will be paid to see that it does. Thousands of learning experiments of varying levels of sophistication have been reported, and you may want to base a paper in this field of study on a mini-experiment that you have done. Just as in child-growth studies, real life experience makes the paper much more significant to you even though many others may have already done the same things.

As you gain experience in experimentation, you will find that there are many factors that have to be controlled if the research is going to be able to be generalized to other populations; however, as a beginner, you can do simple conditioning experiments that help you to know that what you have done has made a difference. This feeling of being able to control what happens in learning is exciting and can help you to become a true experimenter-teacher. Because I think there is more to learning than conditioning, I hope that many of you will carry your experiments along to the point where the learners can see relationships in what you have been conditioning them to do. For instance, if you use behavior modification to increase attention, you should help the student see that attention has in fact been increased and that as a result increased learning has taken place. I even hope that you will help some of the subjects of your conditioning experiments to feel good enough about what has happened that they will try different ways of manipulating the learning situation themselves. If you can do this, you will have been teaching them, if only in a small way, to be creative.

When you write an experimental paper, one for which you have been the experimenter, you will need library background to explain why you did what you did. You will also want to follow certain conventions in reporting your study. We will outline these details later in the book.

TESTS AND MEASUREMENTS

One of the more difficult jobs you will have as a teacher is that of evaluating the progress your students have made. You need the evaluation as feedback about how well you have been teaching, and students and their parents need it as feedback about how well the students are learning. In these days of accountability, school boards and administrators are demanding more and more detailed appraisals of the accomplishments of students. Thus, testing and interpreting the tests will be an important facet of your professional life.

In order to write a paper about tests and measurements, you may have to make up test questions that are then evaluated by your professor. Although it is very difficult to write really good questions, this assignment will usually be quite clear cut and often will not require any elaboration.

No aspect of education has undergone more intense research or been subjected to more intense criticism than has standardized testing. Many of the tests used in schools today are revised forms of tests that have been used for forty or fifty years. You will probably be required to administer some of these tests and interpret the results. In preparation for this task you will want to have read the test manuals, have taken the test yourself, and have administered it at least twice in order to feel sure of your competence. Papers reporting such work are usually highly structured in a way that will be described later in this research guide.

CURRICULUM AND METHODS

In addition to the social foundations—philosophy, history, sociology, economics—and the psychological foundations—growth and development, educational psychology, measurement and evaluation—there are courses in curriculum and methods.

The field of curriculum can be very complex. Decisions have to be made about just what should be taught, at what age, and to whom. At the present time there is an argument about whether boys should have to take home economics in junior high school and whether girls should have to take shop courses. Many of these decisions need to go back to philosophical foundations for rational solutions, but all too often curricular decisions are made for political reasons. Legislators often pass laws requiring everyone to study driver education, drug abuse, or some other subject that has social relevance with little or no thought about the time, money, or training needed by teachers if the programs are to be effective. A major problem concerns how to fit all the things that should be learned into the time the young person spends in school. Such scheduling problems are bound to get worse, because our store of knowledge is doubling every ten years. It seems unrealistic to expect that the brightness of students will accelerate at a similar rate. Thus, increasingly painful choices will have to be made, and you are the people who will have to make them.

More effective instructional systems are being evolved, and, within your own specialty your research in the field of curriculum and instruction will almost certainly focus on determining what these new techniques are. As for using these new techniques, the problems will be similar whether your field is early childhood reading or senior high school mathematics. Assigned papers in these fields are likely to be based on library research supported by field experiences either as an observer, a participant, or a student teacher in an actual classroom setting.

You can see that the education papers you write should be different from those written for such courses as history or political science. You are studying to be a practitioner and not just a master of content. Your classmates may have a major in a parent discipline such as history, or may not have a single college level course in the area being studied. Differences of this magnitude in basic background make it difficult for the professor to adjust class assignments in a wholly satisfactory way. Your own reading and study can help bridge the gaps in presentation.

The world you live in has grown from the experiences you have had. Many of these experiences come from books, but they are more useful to you if they are tied into real-world experiences. That is why I have stressed the need to get out and see students in different settings. Already there is at least the beginning of a generation gap between you and the young people you are going to be teaching. You cannot assume that things are the way they were when you were in school. Your research should help you to broaden your perspective and to expand your horizons to include as much as possible of the world in which your students live.

Later I will discuss various kinds of papers you can write based on a multiplicity of different learning experiences, but for now let us concentrate on the mechanics of paper writing.

Part II

HOW TO RESEARCH A PAPER IN EDUCATION

Selecting, Defining, and Organizing a Topic

As a student in education you have dedicated yourself to becoming an expert teacher. All your energies should be directed to achieving this goal, and all of your research papers should contribute directly to increasing your competence as a professional educator. In large part, the success of your endeavors will depend upon the attitude with which you approach your tasks, which are often chosen for you rather than by you. Still, all of these tasks can help you to develop insights and skills that you will be able to use for the rest of your life. Many of the "facts" that you study and write about today will become myths tomorrow. But your understanding of the new facts that you will confront during the next forty years of your teaching life will have its roots in the materials that you master as you write your research papers.

Often your professor will assign a topic for a paper, or will give you a list of topics from which to choose. This practice is common in beginning courses; however, many faculty members will give you an assignment that is really broad so that you can choose what you are going to do within these outlines. Even when the paper is specified by title, you can handle the topic in many ways.

It will pay you to take time to think before you start writing. Read a textbook on the general field. Read short summary statements such as those in the *Encyclopaedia Britannica* or the *Encyclopedia of Educational Research.* Talk to classmates about the topic, talk to your teaching assistant, and even talk to the professor about the field. This preliminary conversation and reading will give you a feel for the subject, a framework into which you can fit ideas. If you have an open assignment, ask yourself and others "why" questions. Why should I give homework? Why should schools be integrated? Why should children start school at six years of age? Quintilian was raising the last question two thousand years ago. Many educational practices have good reasons behind them. Many of them had reasons that were practical in a largely rural America but which may no longer be valid. Many methods of teaching are based on folklore, and should be questioned. In other words, there are many things about teaching that should be changed, so there are many research projects that need to be done. Some of the most effective papers can come out of questioning the way things have always been done. When you start thinking for yourself, even assigned projects become exciting and growth producing.

READING THE LITERATURE

When you have a broad, general idea of the area in which you want to write your paper, you will need to start serious reading. After you have read a number of articles, chapters, or books, you will redefine your topic. Occasionally this redefinition will mean starting on a new topic, but more often it involves limiting the subject and sharpening the focus of what you are studying so that your paper will have more depth. Even when you are still defining your topic, there are certain mechanics that will save you time if you observe them.

Mechanics in reading include keeping a card record. On the card you should record the bibliographic information that you will need if you want to reference the material. This listing includes the name of the author(s) and the name of the article or book. If the article comes from a journal, include the name of the journal, the volume number, the date, and the pages on which the article appeared. If the material appeared in a book of collected articles, record the name of the editor(s) and the title of the book. You also record the city in which the book was published, the name of the publisher, and the date the book was published. There are many special cases that vary in significant ways from this outline. Most of these are detailed in the section of this volume on bibliography. If you record this data when you are starting to read, you will have it when you need it later to write your paper. I have spent many hours and days searching in the library for a reference because I did not do what I am telling you to do. Just one lost reference that is a bit obscure can take as much time to locate as all the time you spend recording the material for fifty references you do not use later.

System in reading refers to what you should look for and summarize as you read. You will also want to record your own reaction to the reading, but this reaction should be kept separate from the analysis of what the author actually said. The next section discusses ways of recording your reaction. You may want to record your analysis under headings similar to the ones that follow.

1. Topic: What do the authors say they are going to do? The preface is usually quite explicit about the ideas the authors are trying to get across. Often you can decide on the basis of reading the preface whether the book is close enough to your topic to warrant further study. In research papers the topic of the paper is often found under a heading such as "the problem." You will find it useful to state succinctly on your card just what the topic of the paper or book is. By putting this material into your own words, you will be able to remember the idea better when you are trying to fit these ideas into place with other sources you have used.
2. Narrow topic: Examine the material to see just how the authors limited their subject. This restriction is more apparent in a paper or research report than in a book. When you summarize this part of the paper, you may find it helpful to list key terms and their meanings.
3. Data: In your analysis of the writing you will want to summarize the evidence the authors use to make their argument. What experimental results have they re-

ported? What authorities have they used to support their arguments? Often you will want to note inconsistencies in the data. Often different findings by different authors can be traced to the kinds of data they produced. Sometimes you can spot inconsistencies more easily than can people who know the field better than you do. It is common for people who have been working on a topic a long time to have slipped into automatically accepting a way of responding to data because they have been doing it for so long. New people who do not know the conventional wisdom ask questions that later seem obvious, but that have been overlooked by experts. I am reminded of a bridge opponent of mine who said, "If you had played that hand properly, you would not have won." He was quite serious. You have something to give even though you are just starting your career.

4. Discussion of findings: You will want to summarize what the authors say they found if the article is related to research. In a more general article there will usually be a section that mentions what has been discovered.

5. Conclusions: This part of the authors' paper should be distinguished from the discussion. In the discussion the authors are telling what they found in relation to what they set out to explore. In the conclusion the authors tell what they think the findings mean in terms of the subject.

If you make it a habit to record these five topics you will find that you are understanding a great deal more than you did before you started reading in such a critical way. The topic heading will make it possible for you to pull the work of different authors together and review what each of them has said. In all of this summarizing you should be as clear and as unbiased as you can in recording the authors' viewpoint.

Reaction is your own thoughts and feelings about the reading, and it is a most important part of your reading activity. Reaction should be separated from the systematic review of what the authors said. After you have summarized what has been said, you should think about it. You should not just accept what the authors say without fitting their ideas in with other things you have read on the topic. One of the things you might consider is bias. If you are a woman, you will tend to check for bias on a sexist basis. If you are from a minority, you will tend to check for bias against your particular group. It is more difficult to see other kinds of biases, especially those in favor of your viewpoint. This kind of bias seems to be just good judgment. In education many articles are biased by the authors' fundamental assumptions, which often they do not even know they have.

In addition to thinking about authors' biases, you should also consider how this author's work fits in with the other works on this topic that you have read. This is the part of writing a paper that contributes most to your intellectual growth. You are building up your own understanding rather than accepting what someone else says. This creative synthesis is the essence of scholarship, and it is the hope that this synthesis will take place that leads professors to assign papers to you.

To summarize, when you read, record the bibliographic information in the form in which you may need it; summarize the author's presentation by topic, narrow topic, data, discussion, and conclusions; add your own reaction, including obvious biases and also the ways in which this material fits in with other things you know or have read.

Secondary sources will be used often such as textbooks, summaries of research, and similar materials. Record the name and page of the secondary source on a separate card and give credit to this source unless you use the original material that has been quoted. It is always desirable to check the original source; frequently you will be surprised to find that the original does not sound at all like the material that the second author described. Collections of symposium papers or of original papers on a topic are excellent sources of material, and some of the hardest to re-find. As I mentioned earlier, in referencing this material you will need the author you have read and the editor or editors of the book in which the material appeared. Of course, all the rest of the data for the book—publisher, city, and date—need to be recorded. Finally, you need the pages on which the article appears in the volume.

LIMITING THE TOPIC

As you have read and thought about the different ramifications of what you have read, almost certainly you have found many different facets of the general topic. Almost any of them would be worth studying in depth. Many of them are substantial enough to require a lifetime of research and still have room for many years of productive work. Terman spent forty-five years trying to make intelligence tests more accurate. You may have heard that some people are still dissatisfied with what has been done in this rather narrow field. If the experts have worked so long and so hard on a topic, you are not likely to solve it all in a relatively short paper, although you can make a start. If you explore an area in depth, you can become fascinated with the significance of the ideas being developed. I can remember very well a term paper I had to do for a summer session course. I turned the paper in to the professor on time, but I spent the next four years working very hard on aspects of this same topic. I had started the paper only because it was required, but the major portion of the work I did was for my own satisfaction. Not every paper is as challenging, but each can be fascinating and a beginning to a period of intellectual growth.

Narrowing the scope of your paper usually is difficult because so many interesting byways present themselves, and all can be intriguing. Your paper will be better, more scholarly, and of more lasting significance to you if you probe a narrow topic in depth rather than if you try to cover a broader area in a superficial manner. In junior high school, students are taught the theory of relativity in about half an hour. In graduate school a single aspect of this theory can require a year's course. Graduate students are probably more intrigued with their study than is the junior high-school pupil. Your paper should fall somewhere between these extremes. Often you can put aside other important problems for later exploration. For instance, if you are interested in school busing for purposes of school integration you can probably learn more and write a better paper if you study the effect on a single school or school district rather than trying to examine the effect on the country or even on a single state. In the same way, if you are doing a mini-experiment, you will probably learn more by trying to use reinforcement theory to change Johnny's habit of going to the pencil sharpener every five minutes rather than by trying to determine all the ways reinforcement theory can be used in school. The original reading that you would do on either of these topics would provide a framework or an orientation for the later study in depth. This framework should also be included as part of your paper so that the reader knows what you are thinking.

As you read, and sharpen the focus of your study, you will be collecting data to use later either as the basis for the design of an experiment or as supporting data that will help to prove or disprove a hypothesis. The note taking that was outlined earlier is particularly important as you assemble the evidence for and against a case. To some extent you are acting like a lawyer who is investigating both sides of a case in order to arrive at the truth. You will differ from the typical trial lawyer after you know the whole story because you will tell both sides and not just the one that you would like to win. The logic that makes one conclusion sounder than another comes from the data that you assemble. It is a difficult task to look for evidence that points to different kinds of hypotheses, but it is important that you build up this kind of objectivity and that you collect the data that support all sides of the argument—there are seldom just two possible answers.

ORGANIZING THE EVIDENCE

When you actually get down to writing your paper, make it easy for the reader to go through your own report by writing the kind of summary that you have been making of the sources you have been reading. Your title should give a clue to what is presented, but it should be short. Avoid words like "A Study of," "An Investigation of." Since you are doing a paper, it can be assumed that it is a study of something. In general, titles are better if they start with key words that can be used as locator words. It is unlikely that the paper you are writing at this stage of your career will be indexed, but some later ones probably will be. In these days of computer searches, initial words that show the meaning of the paper are useful. This topic will be pursued further in the section on writing the report.

In your organization start with a precise statement of what you have done and why. Go on to be quite specific about the limitations of your topic; then present the data on both sides and draw the conclusions that seem warranted by the evidence.

As you read, collect your data so that you can use it in this way. If you keep thinking about the significance of what you are reading, of where it fits, you will find writing the report comparatively easy. The hard part is thinking about the evidence and seeing how the pieces fit. Once this analysis has been done, all you have to do is write it down in an orderly manner.

Using the Library

In chapter 2 I discussed reading the literature. In this section I will deal with using the library to find the material you will need. Libraries are growing more complex—adding records, pictures, films, maps, and other materials to the books, journals, and pamphlets they have always had. The card catalogs are resources of great value for finding materials. They contain author, title, and subject listings. In many libraries all of these cards are filed in a single alphabetical list, but in other, usually larger, libraries, the lists are filed separately. The subject listings can be particularly helpful in getting started on a topic, because they will bring to your attention many books that you had not learned about in your preliminary reading.

One of the difficulties in using the library is finding the journal articles that are most germane to your topic. An explanation of how these can be located most efficiently will follow the discussion on finding your way around the book collections. Even if your paper is primarily an observation of children in different situations, or an experimental study, you will need to review the relevant literature to put your observations into perspective or to help define exactly what your experiment should be.

Practically every library in the United States uses one of two classification systems—the Dewey decimal system or the Library of Congress classification. Both systems put books on the same topic together. For instance, books on the neurology of learning appear under general areas of neurology, physiology, learning, and memory. Both systems are described below.

DEWEY DECIMAL CLASSIFICATION

Melvil Dewey worked out this approach in the latter part of the nineteenth century. The Dewey decimal classification system divides all knowledge, as represented by books and other materials that are acquired by libraries, into nine main classes numbered 1 to 9. Material too general to belong to any one of these classes, such as newspapers and encyclopedias, falls into a tenth class, numbered 0, which precedes the others. The classes are expressed in hundreds; thus, 000 is general works, 100 is philosophy, 200 is religion, 300 is social sciences, and so on. Each division is subdivided into nine sections preceded by a general section; thus, 370 is education in general, 372 is elementary education, and 376 is education of women. Further division to bring together similar materials is accomplished by the addition of digits following a decimal point. Most numbers do not exceed six digits in length, i.e., do not extend more than three to the right of the decimal point; however, there are cases of numbers extending to nine and sometimes even more digits. The description of the education series from 370.000 to 379.999 takes 40 pages in Dewey decimal classification.

The basic classification system ranges from 000 to 999:

000-099   General works
100-199   Philosophy
200-299   Religion
300-399   Social sciences
400-499   Language
500-599   Pure sciences
600-699   Technology
700-799   Arts
800-899   Literature
900-999   History

The major divisions for education are as follows:

370.1   Philosophy, theories, principles
370.7   Study and teaching of education
371   The school
372-374   Levels of education and schools

375	Programs of studies
376	Education of women
377	Schools and religion
378	Higher education—the breakdown under this topic will illustrate the way subdivisions are made
378.11	Administrative personnel
.12	Faculty
.14	College year
.15	Types and levels of institutions
.16	Educational measurement and student placement
.17	Methods of instruction and study
.18	School discipline
.19	Other aspects

You can see that there is great precision in the process of classifying books and other publications.

LIBRARY OF CONGRESS CLASSIFICATION

The Library of Congress classification system was adopted in 1900, three years after the Library of Congress moved from the Capitol to its new building. It changed methods in order to have a more systematic and functional arrangement.

This system divides the fields of knowledge into twenty groups. It assigns a letter to each and combines arabic numerals and additional letters to separate the main groups into classes and subclasses in somewhat the same way used in the Dewey decimal system. All books are divided into the following basic groups:

A	General works. Polygraphy	H	Social sciences
B	Philosophy. Psychology. Religion	J	Political science
		K	Law
C	Auxiliary sciences of history	L	Education
D	History: General and Old World	M	Music and books on music
E-F	History: America	N	Fine arts
G	Geography. Anthropology. Recreation	P	Language and literature
		Q	Science

R	Medicine	V	Naval science
S	Agriculture	Z	Bibliography and
T	Technology		library science
U	Military science		

Education

For our purposes the categories under L are the most important. The following are the major subdivisions under L:

L   General works
LA History of education
LB Theory and practice of education. Teaching
Preschool, kindergarten, primary, elementary, secondary, higher

1051-1140	Educational psychology and child study
1705-2285	Education and training of teachers
2503-3095	School administration, organization, discipline, etc.
3205-3325	School architecture and equipment
3401-3497	School hygiene
3525-3635	Special days, school life, etc.

LC Special forms, relations and applications

8-63	Special forms of education
	Self culture; home, private, and public education
71-245	Sociological aspects of education
	Education and the state, secularization, etc.
129-145	Compulsory education. Attendance
149-160	Illiteracy
221-235	Schools as social centers
251-951	Character education. Religion and education. Education under church control
1001-1261	Types of education: Humanistic, vocational, professional, etc.
1390-5140	Education of special classes of persons
	Women, Negroes, exceptional children, defectives, etc.

5201-6691   Education extension. Adult education
Universities and colleges
LD   United States
LE   Other American
LF   Europe
LG   Asia, Africa, Oceania
LH   University, college, and school magazines, etc.
LJ   College fraternities and their publications
LT   Textbooks [Only textbooks covering several subjects are
classified here. Textbooks of particular subjects are
classified with those in subjects in B-Z.]

In addition to the card catalog there are indices, abstracts,
and guides that can be of great help to you in finding material
for your paper. In education there are over seven hundred
journals of one kind or another that deal primarily or
peripherally with topics you might be interested in studying. In
addition there are a great many research reports, conference
papers, teacher guides, and curriculum materials that might be
important to you, depending on your topic. You need help just
finding and learning to use the indices that enable you to
discover what is available.

Once you have your library numbers, you are in a position
to start serious reading and note taking. Make sure you have
made complete bibliographic notations including the pages on
which chapters or articles appear. Check off your bibliographic
reference list as you read the articles. After reading make your
own summary of the main points covered and their significance
to your topic. This process of summarizing will help you keep
the different materials separated and clear in your mind. If a
particular journal seems to have a concentration of items on the
topic in which you are interested, you may want to look at
more recent issues of the same journal. Since it takes about six
months before a journal's contents get into the abstracts—and
often the period is much longer than that—the latest material on
a topic may not yet be indexed.

Depending on the state of your finances, you may find it
easier to make machine copies of critical selections than to copy

them by hand. Your books and journal articles will refer to other articles you may or may not already have listed. Some of them should be added to your own list for further research.

As time goes on and you write papers in different courses, you should become familiar with all of the different resources. Following sections describe (1) ERIC, (2) Education Index, (3) Psychological Abstracts, (4) Child Development Abstracts and Bibliography, (5) Sociological Abstracts, (6) Sociology of Education Abstracts, and (7) Buros Mental Measurement Yearbooks.

ERIC—EDUCATIONAL RESOURCES INFORMATION CENTER

ERIC is now the most important source of information about topics in education. The system is still growing but it has become stabilized. Now most, but not all, of the material indexed and abstracted in the other sources is included in ERIC. Since ERIC is rather new, articles and papers published before 1969 may not be listed; therefore, other sources should be consulted. ERIC consists of two main parts, which are independent but complementary systems: RIE, Research in Education, and CIJE, Current Index to Journals in Education. RIE makes unpublished materials available, and CIJE is a source of information about published materials. RIE was established several years before CIJE.

ERIC was started as a way of making all the research studies available to the educational community. Many of these studies had been supported by the Office of Education in the Department of Health, Education, and Welfare, but there was no easy means of locating them, reproducing them, or organizing them. It was decided that a system should be organized so that a computer could find items. Computer searches work best when the vocabulary is as restricted as possible, so a thesaurus was constructed that made it possible to translate synonyms and similar ideas into words that were used for coding. Obviously you must learn to use the thesaurus. An enormous volume of reports and papers are written in education each year. To break up the work of organizing the material, a system of clearinghouses was established at universities and the headquarters of professional associations. Each clearinghouse is concerned with a specific topic. As this book is being written, there are sixteen clearinghouses with delegated responsibility, as shown on Table 1.

Research in Education (RIE)

Research in Education is the medium through which ERIC brings technical reports, research reports, speeches and "papers presented at," program descriptions, teacher guides, statistical compilations, and curriculum materials to the attention of the wider educational community. The material is presented in the form of a monthly journal with six parts: Document Résumés, Subject Index, Author Index, Institution Index, Accession Number Cross Reference Index, and New Thesaurus Terms. Semiannual and Annual Cumulative Indices are also available. These are published with each part in a different volume.

Document Résumés is one of the most useful parts of the journal. In addition to full bibliographic referencing as shown in Figure 1, there is an abstract of the contents of the material. The résumés are listed alphabetically by clearinghouse so that all the items on early childhood are together, as are all those on the disadvantaged. In this way you are able to skim a large number of items in a field in a short time. In many colleges and universities, microfiches of all the items abstracted are received and are available for study. Take the ED number to the file, pick out the 4″ by 6″ piece of plastic in its paper holder and feed it into the microfiche reader. On this sheet there are up to 96 pages of the original document, and you can move from the résumé to the full document quickly.

Subject Index (Figure 2) lists the articles by the major subject terms listed in the *Thesaurus of ERIC Descriptors*. The same article will show up a number of times under different descriptor terms. Usually no more than five such listings are made for any one article. The items are listed in alphabetical order by title, and they also give the ED number, which makes it possible to find the résumé quickly. If you have a subject in

TABLE 1 / ERIC Clearinghouses

The ERIC Clearinghouses have responsibility within the network for acquiring the significant educational literature within their particular areas, selecting the highest quality and most relevant material, processing (i.e., cataloging, indexing, abstracting) the selected items for input to the data base, and also for providing information analysis products and various user services based on the data base.

The exact number of Clearinghouses has fluctuated over time in response to the shifting needs of the educational community. There are currently 16 Clearinghouses. These are listed below, together with full addresses, telephone numbers, and brief scope notes describing the areas they cover.

ERIC Clearinghouse in Career Education

Northern Illinois University
College of Education
204 Gurler School
DeKalb, Illinois 60115
Telephone: (815) 753-1251 or 1252

Career education, formal and informal at all levels, encompassing attitudes, self-knowledge, decision-making skills, general and occupational knowledge, and specific vocational and occupational skills; adult and continuing education, formal and informal, relating to occupational, family, leisure, citizen, organizational, and retirement roles; vocational and technical education, including new sub-professional fields, industrial arts, and vocational rehabilitation for the handicapped.

ERIC Clearinghouse on Counseling and Personnel Services

University of Michigan
School of Education Bldg., Rm. 2108
E. University & S. University Sts.
Ann Arbor, Michigan 48104
Telephone: (313) 764-9492

Preparation, practice, and supervision of counselors at all educational levels and in all settings; theoretical development of counseling and guidance; use and results of personnel procedures such as testing, interviewing, disseminating, and analyzing such information; group work and case work; nature of pupil, student, and adult characteristics; personnel workers and their relation to career planning, family consultations, and student orientation activities.

ERIC Clearinghouse on Urban Education

U. D. Disadvantaged
Box 40, 525 W. 120th Street
Teachers College
Columbia University
New York, New York 10027

Covers the effects of disadvantaged experiences and environments, from birth onward; academic, intellectual, and social performance of disadvantaged children and youth from grade 3 through college entrance; programs and practices which provide learning experiences designed to compensate for special problems of disadvantaged; issues, programs, and practices related to economic and ethnic discrimination, segregation, desegregation, and integration in education; issues, programs, and materials related to redressing the curriculum imbalance in the treatment of ethnic minority groups.

ERIC Clearinghouse on Early Childhood Education

University of Illinois
College of Education
805 W. Pennsylvania Avenue
Urbana, Illinois 61801
Telephone: (217) 333-1386

Prenatal factors; parental behavior; the physical, psychological, social, educational, and cultural development of children from birth through the primary grades; educational theory, research, and practice related to the development of young children.

ERIC Clearinghouse on Educational Management

University of Oregon
Eugene, Oregon 97403
Telephone: (503) 686-5043

Leadership, management, and structure of public and private educational organizations; practice and theory of administration; preservice and inservice preparation of administrators, tasks, and processes of administration; methods and varieties of organization, organizational change, and social context of the organization.

Sites, buildings, and equipment for education; planning, financing, constructing, renovating, equipping, maintaining, operating, insuring, utilizing, and evaluating educational facilities.

ERIC Clearinghouse on Handicapped and Gifted Children

The Council for Exceptional Children
1920 Association Drive
Reston, Va. 22091
Telephone: (703) 620-3660

Aurally handicapped, visually handicapped, mentally handicapped, physically handicapped, emotionally disturbed, speech handicapped, learning disabilities, and the gifted; behavioral, psychomotor, and communication disorders, administration of special education services; preparation and continuing education of professional and paraprofessional personnel; preschool learning and development of the exceptional; general studies on creativity.

ERIC Clearinghouse on Higher Education

The George Washington University
One Dupont Circle, Suite 630
Washington, D.C. 20036
Telephone: (202) 296-2597

Various subjects relating to college and university students, college and university conditions and problems, college and university programs. Curricular and instructional problems and programs, faculty, institutional research. Federal programs, professional education (medical, law, etc.), graduate education, university extension programs, teaching-learning, planning, governance, finance, evaluation, interinstitutional arrangements, and management of higher educational institutions.

ERIC Clearinghouse on Information Resources

Stanford University
School of Education
Center for Research and Development in Teaching
Stanford, California 94305
Telephone: (415) 321-2300 ext. 3345

Management, operation, and use of libraries; the technology to improve their operation and the education, training, and professional activities of librarians and information specialists. Educational techniques involved in microteaching, systems analysis, and programmed instruction employing audiovisual teaching aids and technology, such as television, radio, computers, and films. Technology in society adaptable to education, including cable television, communication satellites, microforms, and public television.

ERIC Clearinghouse for Junior Colleges

University of California
Powell Library, Room 96
405 Hilgard Avenue
Los Angeles, California 90024
Telephone: (213) 825-3931

Development, administration, and evaluation of public and private community junior colleges. Junior college students, staff, curricula, programs, libraries, and community services.

ERIC Clearinghouse on Languages and Linguistics

Modern Language Assoc. of America
62 Fifth Avenue
New York, New York 10011
Telephone: (212) 741-7863

Languages and linguistics. Instructional methodology, psychology of language learning, cultural and intercultural content, application of linguistics, curricular problems and developments, teacher training and qualifications, language sciences, psycho-linguistics, theoretical and applied linguistics, language pedagogy, bilingualism, and commonly and uncommonly taught languages including English for speakers of other languages.

ERIC Clearinghouse for Reading and Communication Skills

Nat'l. Council of Teachers of English
1111 Kenyon Road
Urbana, Illinois 61801
Telephone: (217) 328-3870

Reading, English, and communication skills, preschool through college. Educational research and development in reading, writing, speaking, and listening. Identification, diagnosis, and remediation of reading problems. Speech communication—forensics, mass communication, interpersonal and small group interaction, interpretation, rhetorical and communication theory, instruction development, speech sciences, and theater. Preparation of instructional staff and related personnel in these areas.

All aspects of reading behavior with emphasis on physiology, psychology, sociology, and teaching. Instructional materials, curricula, tests and measurement, preparation of reading teachers and specialists, and methodology at all levels. Role of libraries and other agencies in fostering and guiding reading. Diagnostic and remedial services in school and clinical settings.

ERIC Clearinghouse on Rural Education and Small Schools

New Mexico State University
Box 3AP
Las Cruces, New Mexico 88003
Telephone: (505) 646-2623

Education of Indian Americans, Mexican Americans, Spanish Americans, and migratory farm workers and their children; outdoor education; economic, cultural, social, or other factors related to educational programs in rural areas and small schools; disadvantaged of rural and small school populations.

ERIC Clearinghouse on Science, Mathematics, and Environmental Education

Ohio State University
1800 Cannon Drive
400 Lincoln Tower
Columbus, Ohio 43210
Telephone: (614) 422-6717

All levels of science, mathematics, and environmental education; development of curriculum and instructional materials; media applications; impact of interest, intelligence, values, and concept development upon learning; preservice and inservice teacher education and supervision.

ERIC Clearinghouse for Social Studies/Social Science Education

855 Broadway
Boulder, Colorado 80302
Telephone: (303) 443-1383 ext. 8434

All levels of social studies and social science; all activities relating to teachers; content of disciplines; applications of learning theory, curriculum theory, child development theory, and instructional theory; research and development programs; special needs of student groups; education as a social science; social studies/social science and the community.

ERIC Clearinghouse on Teacher Education

American Association of Colleges for Teacher Education
One Dupont Circle, Suite 616
Washington, D.C. 20036
Telephone: (202) 293-7280

School personnel at all levels; all issues from selection through preservice and inservice preparation and training to retirement; curricula; educational theory and philosophy; general education not specifically covered by Educational Management Clearinghouse; Title XI NDEA Institutes not covered by subject specialty in other ERIC Clearinghouses; all aspects of physical education.

ERIC Clearinghouse on Tests, Measurement, and Evaluation

Educational Testing Service
Princeton, New Jersey 08540
Telephone: (609) 921-9000 ext. 2691

Tests and other measurement devices; evaluation procedures and techniques; application of tests, measurement, or evaluation in educational projects or programs.

Source: Mock-Up ERIC, 1974.

ERIC Accession Number—identification number sequentially assigned to documents as they are processed.

Author(s).

Title.

Organization where document originated.

Date published.

Contract or Grant Number—contract numbers have OEC prefixes; grant numbers have OEG prefixes.

Alternate source for obtaining documents.

EDRS Price—price through ERIC Document Reproduction Service. "MF" means microfiche; "HC" means hard copy. When listed "not available from EDRS" other sources are cited above.

Legislative Authority Code for identifying the legislation which supported the research activity (when applicable). *

Clearinghouse accession number.

Sponsoring Agency—agency responsible for initiating, funding, and managing the research project.

Report Number and/or Bureau Number—assigned by originator.

Descriptive Note.

Descriptors—subject terms which characterize substantive contents. Only the major terms, preceded by an asterisk, are printed in the subject index.

Identifiers—additional identifying terms not found in the Thesaurus of ERIC Descriptors.

Informative Abstract.

Abstractor's initials.

ED 013 371   64   AA 000 223
Norberg, Kenneth D.
Iconic Signs and Symbols in Audiovisual Communication, an Analytical Survey of Selected Writings and Research Findings, Final Report.
Sacramento State Coll., Calif.
Spons Agency—USOE Bur. of Research
Report No.—NDEA-VIIB-449
Pub Date—15 Apr 66
Contract—OEC-4-16-023
Note—129 p; Speech given before the 22nd National Conference on Higher Education, Chicago, Ill., 7 Mar 66.
Available from—Indiana University Press, 10th and Morton St., Bloomington, Indiana 47401 ($2.95)
EDRS Price MF-$0.65 HC-$6.58
Descriptors—*Bibliographies, *Communication (thought transfer), *Perception, *Pictorial Stimuli, *Symbolic Language, Instructional Technology, Visual Stimuli.
Identifiers—Stanford Binet Test, Wechsler Intelligence Scale; Lisp 1.5; Cupertino Union School District.

The field of analogic, or iconic, signs was explored to (1) develop an annotated bibliography and (2) prepare an analysis of the subject area. The scope of the study was limited to only those components of messages, instructional materials, and communicative stimuli that can be described properly as iconic. The author based the study on a definition of an iconic sign as one that looks like the thing it represents. The bibliography was intended to be representative and reasonably comprehensive and to give emphasis to current research. The analysis explored the nature of iconic signs as reflected in the literature and research.
(AL)

Figure 1 Sample Entry for *Document Resumes*/RIE (From *Research in Education*, Level 2, Mock-Up ERIC, page 5.)

mind, you will want to check it in the *Thesaurus* to make sure another similar term is not the one you should be using.

Author Index (Figure 3) gives you an alphabetical listing of authors by their last names. Included are the titles of the articles and the ED number. In many cases if you have found an article by an author that impresses you, further reading of what he or she has done would be helpful. By means of the Author Index you can go directly to the work.

Institution Index (Figure 4) will probably be less useful to you except to see what has been produced in your own institution. The listing is alphabetical by the institution, but sometimes a bit of searching is necessary. For example, the University of California, Santa Barbara is listed: California, University, Santa Barbara.

Accession Number Cross Reference Index is a part of the volume that you will not be likely to use until you reach a highly sophisticated level of research. It provides a way of finding the ED number when all you have available is the clearinghouse number. Normally only those who have been

Perception
Iconic Signs and Symbols in Audiovisual Communication, an Analytical Survey of Selected Writings and Research Findings, Final Report.

ED 013 371

Accession Number ————————————

Figure 2 Sample Subject Index/RIE (from *Research in Education*, Level 2, Mock-Up ERIC, page 17.)

Norberg, Kenneth D.
Iconic Signs and Symbols in Audiovisual Communication, An Analytical
Survey of Selected Writings and Research Findings, Final Report.

                                                              ED 013 371
                              Accession Number —————————

Figure 3 Sample Author Index/RIE (From *Research in Education*, Level 2,
Mock-Up ERIC, page 21.)

Sacramento State College, Calif.
Iconic Signs and Symbols in Audiovisual Communication, An Analytical
Survey of Selected Writings and Research Findings, Final Report.

                                                              ED 013 371
                              Accession Number —————————

Figure 4 Sample Institution Index/RIE (From *Research in Education*,
Level 2, Mock-Up ERIC, page 311.)

using materials directly from the clearinghouse and wish to locate the material in the Document File will use this source.

New Thesaurus Terms, generated as they are needed, are reviewed, given a place in the system, and added to those already available in the bound copy of the *Thesaurus*.

Current Index to Journals in Education (CIJE)

The older *Education Index* covered a wide band of sources, but many minor publications were not included. The CIJE, published monthly and much like the RIE, covers over seven hundred journals, many of which are peripheral to education but which contain articles relevant to the work of researchers in education. CIJE has been published since January 1969. The articles that are indexed are not available in microfiche as are the reports in the RIE, but since they are published, they are available in the regular journal literature. In many ways you will find the material in CIJE more useful to you than that in RIE, which tends to be much more specialized.

The CIJE is divided into four main sections, which become separate volumes in the annual publication: the Main Entry section, the Subject Index, Author Index, and Journal Contents Index. The Main Entry section contains a full bibliographic reference, descriptors, including those that are used in the Subject Index, identifiers that are not found in the Subject Index and an annotation (Figure 5). The Main Entry section is arranged alphabetically within 52 descriptor groups. These groups, which are listed below, make it possible for you to search for articles of interest to you in much the same way that grouping by clearinghouses helped in searching the RIE.

The Subject Index and the Author Index are similar to the related indices in RIE. In addition, there is a Journal Contents Index, which makes it possible to see what other related articles might be in a particular journal issue. There is a four to six month lag between journal publication and the appearance of the contents in CIJE. Figures 6, 7, 8 illustrate how to read the Subject Index, the Author Index, and the Journal Title Index.

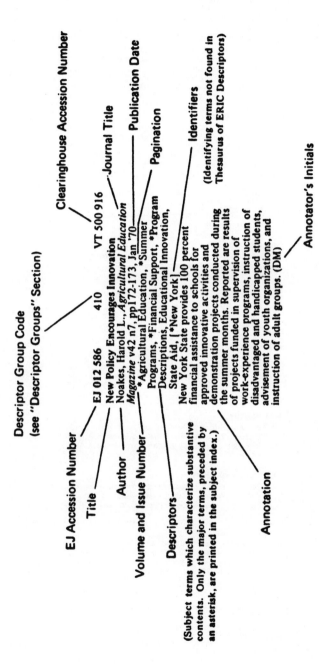

Descriptor Group Code
(see "Descriptor Groups" Section)

Clearinghouse Accession Number

Journal Title

Publication Date

Pagination

Identifiers

(Identifying terms not found in
Thesaurus of ERIC Descriptors)

Annotator's Initials

EJ Accession Number

Title

Author

Volume and Issue Number

Descriptors

(Subject terms which characterize substantive
contents. Only the major terms, preceded by
an asterisk, are printed in the subject index.)

Annotation

EJ 012 586   410   VT 500 916

New Policy Encourages Innovation
Noakes, Harold L., *Agricultural Education
Magazine* v42 n7, pp172-173, Jan '70
*Agricultural Education, *Summer
Programs, *Financial Support, *Program
Descriptions, Educational Innovation,
State Aid. [*New York]
New York State provides 100 percent
financial assistance to schools for
approved innovative activities and
demonstration projects conducted during
the summer months. Reported are results
of projects funded in supervision of
work-experience programs, instruction of
disadvantaged and handicapped students,
advisement of youth organizations, and
instruction of adult groups. (DM)

Figure 5 Sample Main Entry/CIJE (From *Current Index to Journals in Education*, Mock-Up ERIC, page 6.)

DESCRIPTOR GROUPS

010 Abilities
Intelligence and performance of individuals, e.g., Academic Aptitude, etc. Also contained herein are specific skills as they relate to the ability for acquiring and performing given skills, knowledge of the means or methods for accomplishing a task. For skill-related occupations, *see* OCCUPATIONS.

020 Administration
Management and management-related processes in administering various types of school plants and educational organizations. For different types of administrative personnel, *see* PERSONNEL AND GROUPS. For program development, *see* FINANCE. For financial factors, *see* FINANCE. *See also* PROGRAMS.

030 Arts
Fine Arts, Theater Arts, Painting, Freehand Drawing, Sculpture, Music, Ceramics, Graphic Arts, Dramatics, etc. *See also* HUMANITIES.

040 Attitudes
Attitudes of individuals or groups toward a given object or condition, e.g., Student Attitudes, Class Attitudes, Personal Interests, Values, etc.

050 Audiovisual Materials and Methods
Audiovisual materials and methods used for instructional purposes, e.g., Closed Circuit Television, Mass Media. *See also* COMMUNICATION, EQUIPMENT.

060 Behavior
Kinds and types of human behavior and factors related to the study of behavior, e.g., Violence, Socially Deviant Behavior, Conditioned Response, Overt Response, etc. *See also* LEARNING AND COGNITION, PSYCHOLOGY, SOCIOLOGY.

070 Biology
Study of life including Zoology and Botany, e.g., Ecology, Heredity, Plant Science, Animal Science, Physiology, Neurology, etc. *See also* HEALTH AND SAFETY.

080 Communication
Methods and characteristics of communication, e.g., Oral Expression, Verbal Communication, etc. For types of communication equipment, *see also* EQUIPMENT.

090 Counseling
Counseling Programs, Counseling Services, Guidance Programs, Guidance Services, Individual Counseling, Group Counseling, Vocational Counseling, etc. *See also* ADMINISTRATION, ATTITUDES, BEHAVIOR, PSYCHOLOGY.

100 Culture
Specific cultures, e.g., African Culture, and culture-related factors, e.g., Cultural Differences, Ethnic Grouping, Urban Culture, etc. *See also* RACE RELATIONS.

110 Curriculum
Specific types of curriculum and specific types of courses, e.g., Business English, Elementary Science, Fused Curriculum, Correspondence Courses, Inservice Courses, etc.

120 Demography

Studies related to population including statistical, social and economic factors, e.g., Census Figures, Geographic Distribution, Migration, Population Trends, Student Distribution, Urban Population, etc.

130 Development

Includes stages of growth, the development of specific materials, and the development of education programs, e.g., Childhood Material Development, Program Development, etc. *See also* ADMINISTRATION, BIOLOGY.

140 Education

General education concepts, specific types of education, e.g., Cooperative Education, Educational Improvement, Art Education, Mathematics Education, Music Education, Vocational Education, etc.

150 Employment

Employment, job processes and labor, e.g., Youth Employment, Employment Practices, Job Analysis, Labor Conditions, Labor Unions, Personnel Data, Unemployment, etc. For specific occupations, *see* OCCUPATIONS. *See also* PERSONNEL AND GROUPS.

160 Environment

Aggregate of conditions or influences on communities, schools, culture, and social factors, e.g., Community Influence, Classroom Environment, Cultural Environment, Social Environment, etc. *See also* CULTURE, SOCIOLOGY.

170 Equipment

Instructional equipment and general school and classroom equipment, e.g., Filmstrip Projectors, Tape Recorders, Building Equipment, Classroom Furniture, Vending Machines, etc. *See also* AUDIOVISUAL MATERIALS AND METHODS, FACILITIES.

180 Evaluation

Judgment of processes and people in the education system, e.g., Counseling Effectiveness, Cognitive Measurement, Educational Testing, Student Evaluation, Teacher Evaluation, Test Interpretation. Descriptors that describe the products of evaluation techniques should be applied to the group EVALUATION TECHNIQUES.

190 Evaluation Techniques

Specific techniques or methods used in educational processes for evaluation and comparison of the effectiveness of the education system, e.g., Comparative Testing, Forced Choice Technique, Q Sort, Self Evaluation, etc. *See also* EVALUATION, PSYCHOLOGY, TESTS.

200 Experience

Knowledge or acquired skills, e.g., Emotional Experience, Learning Experience, Social Experience, Teacher Experience, etc. *See also* ABILITIES, ATTITUDES, DEVELOPMENT.

210 Facilities

Buildings, installations, and appendages designed to serve a specific function, e.g., Art Centers, Auditoriums, Crafts Rooms, Dormitories, Lighting, Parks, Public Facilities, Rural Clinics, School Space, Self Contained Classrooms, etc. *See also* EQUIPMENT.

220 Finance

Relating or pertaining to money matters and transaction, e.g., Bond Issues, Expenditures, Fiscal Capacity, Minimum Wage, Salaries, Scholarships, State Aid, Tax Allocation, Welfare, etc. *See also* ADMINISTRATION, GOVERNMENT.

230 Government

Executive, legislative, and judicial aspects of federal state, and local government, e.g., Federal Government, Federal Legislation, Federal Courts, State Government, State Legislation, City Government, Community Agencies (Public), Taxes, etc. *See also* ADMINISTRATION, FINANCE.

240 Handicapped

Limited to persons with or conditions related to physiological or psychological impairments such as Blind, Aurally Handicapped, Partially Sighted, etc.

250 Health and Safety

The physical condition, preservation, or control of an organism or its parts such as Accident Prevention, Family Health, Medical Service, Traffic Safety, and Diseases. *See also* BIOLOGY.

260 Humanities

Branches of learning having primarily a cultural character usually including Literature, History, and Philosophy. *See also* ARTS, CULTURE, LANGUAGE AND SPEECH.

270 Instruction

Activities, materials, and guidance that facilitate learning in either formal or informal situations such as Academic Enrichment, Assignments, Computer Oriented Programs, Correspondence Study, Workshops, etc. *See also* CURRICULUM, EDUCATION, AUDIOVISUAL MATERIALS AND METHODS.

280 Instructional Program Divisions

Any segment of or grouping of students such as Ability Grouping, Age Grade Placement, Nongraded Classes, Grade 1, Grade 2, Grade 3, etc. *See also* ADMINISTRATION.

290 Language and Speech

The study of language includes Morphology (Languages), Phonology, and Syntax. *See also* HUMANITIES. Includes also oral communication such as speech sounds and gesture, e.g., Diction, Phonetic Analysis, Pronunciation, Speech Habits, Speech Therapy, Vowels, etc. *See also* LANGUAGES.

300 Languages

For specific languages and language groups, e.g., Czech, African Languages, English, etc. *See also* COMMUNICATION.

310 Learning and Cognition

The process of acquiring knowledge or skills through study, instruction, or experience such as in Creative Thinking, Discovery Processes, Thought Processes, etc.

320 Library Materials

Includes library collections such as Books, Annotated Bibliographies, Historical Reviews, etc. *See also* AUDIOVISUAL MATERIALS AND METHODS, COMMUNICATION.

330 Library Science

The principles and practices related to processing conducted in the library as well as related user requirements and services, e.g., Abstracting, Information Dissemination, Library Services, etc.

340 Mathematics

Operations and processes involved in the solution of mathematical problems such as Operations Research, Statistics, Algebra, etc.

350 Occupations

One's usual or principal work especially as a means of earning a living, e.g., Farm Occupations, Office Occupations, etc., as well as any study or result of that study, e.g., Occupational Clusters, Occupational Surveys, etc. *See also* EMPLOYMENT, and PERSONNEL AND GROUPS.

360 Opportunities

Advantageous circumstance or combination of circumstances when effecting security, wealth, education, or freedom. Specific opportunities would include Career Opportunities, Teaching Benefits, Housing Opportunities, etc.

370 Organizations (Groups)

A group of persons that has more or less a constant membership, a body of officers, a purpose, and usually a set of regulations such as Advisory Committees, Citizens Councils, Clubs, Housing Industry, etc. *See also* PERSONNEL AND GROUPS.

380 Personnel and Groups

Persons considered together as being related in some manner or having some common characteristics, Accountants, Advanced Students, etc. Also includes a number of things or persons ranged or considered together as being related in some manner having common bonds, e.g., Age Groups, Delinquents, Anglo Americans, Middle Aged, Young Adults, Senior Citizens, College Freshmen, etc. *See also* EMPLOYMENT and SOCIOLOGY. For specific occupations, *see* OCCUPATIONS.

390 Physical Education and Recreation

Activity in which persons refresh themselves mentally or physically, such as in Community Recreation Programs, Social Recreation Programs, etc.

400 Physical Sciences

Study of nonliving materials, e.g., Electricity, Matter, Space, Time, Physics, etc.

410 Programs

A plan or procedure: a schedule or system under which action may be taken towards a desired goal such as After School Programs, College Programs, Work Experience Programs, Youth Programs, etc. *See also* ADMINISTRATION.

420 Psychology

The study of mental phenomena, activities, and processes, e.g., Aggression, Conflict, Fear, Intelligence Factors, Student Adjustment, etc. Also includes psychological forms of treatment, e.g., Role Playing, Sociodrama, etc.

430 Race Relations

Relations among members of different races and methods of affecting such relations, e.g., Classroom Integration, Integration Methods, Racial Balance, Racism, etc. *See also* CULTURE, SOCIOLOGY.

440 Reading

The action or practice of one who reads or the oral Reading, Reading Assignments, Elective Reading, Group Reading, Readability, etc. Also includes reading facility, e.g., Reading, Ability, Reading Failure, Illiteracy, etc. *See also* ABILITIES, COMMUNICATION, and INSTRUCTION.

450 Research

Areas and methods of investigation or experimentation having for its aim the discovery of new facts, e.g., Area Studies, Deaf Research, Experimental Programs, Research Methodology, etc.

460 Resources

Source of supply, support or aid, such as Community Resources, Educational Resources, Natural Resources, etc.

470 Schools

Institutions offering defined studies at defined levels, e.g., Catholic Elementary Schools, Day Schools, High Schools, etc.

480 Social Sciences

Study of the functioning of human society and with the inter-personal relationships of individuals as members of society such as Behavioral Sciences, Communism, Economic Progress, Social Relations. *See also* BEHAVIOR, SOCIOLOGY, RACE RELATIONS

490 Sociology

A broad Social Science which deals with the study of the structure of society, its groups, institutions, and culture, primarily interested in the way people organize themselves into groups, social classes, and institutions such as Anti Segregation Programs, Church Role, Delinquency Causes, Family Characteristics, etc. *See also* SOCIAL SCIENCES, ORGANIZATIONS (GROUPS), RACE RELATIONS.

500 Standards

Morals, ethics, habits, requirements, etc., established by authority, custom, or an individual as acceptable, e.g., Academic Standards, Behavior Standards, Certification, Educational Specifications, Graduation Requirements, Living Standards, State Standards, Teacher Certification, etc.

510 Techniques

Processes, manipulations, or procedures required in any art, study activity, or production, e.g., Classroom Games, Classroom Techniques, Creative Teaching, Educational Methods, Field Trips, Lesson Plans, Methodology, Optional Branching, Production Techniques, Tutoring, etc.

520 Tests

Devices or procedures for measuring ability, achievement, interest, etc., e.g., Achievement Tests, Aptitude Tests, Cognitive Tests, Interest Tests, Language Tests, Multiple Choice Test, Problem Test, Reading Test, Talent Identification, Test Validity, etc.

Source: *Current Index to Journals in Education*, Level 3, Mock-Up ERIC, pages 7, 8, 9.

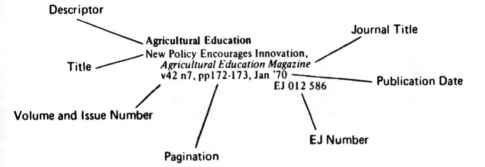

Figure 6 Sample Subject Index/CIJE. A journal article may be listed under as many as five descriptors in the subject index. These descriptors are preceded by an asterisk (*) in the applicable main entry. The complete journal citation is given with each title listed under the descriptor. (From *Current Index to Journals in Education*, Level 3, Mock-Up ERIC, page 5.)

Thesaurus of ERIC Descriptors

I have already mentioned a number of times the need for the *Thesaurus* if you are to be able to use the ERIC system to best advantage. You should be aware that the list of terms accepted for descriptors grows as the need for new terms is demonstrated by usage. One of the principal ways of using the *Thesaurus* is to identify listed terms that are synonyms or near-synonyms for

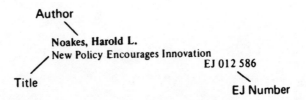

Author

Noakes, Harold L.
New Policy Encourages Innovation
EJ 012 586

Title

EJ Number

Figure 7 Sample Author Index/CIJE. Authors' names are given in full when available. If coauthors are responsible for the article, both names are indexed. If more than two authors are given with the article, only the first author is indexed. (From *Current Index to Journals in Education*, Level 3, Mock-Up ERIC, page 5.)

commonly used words. For instance the *Thesaurus* lists *Guidance Objectives*; related, but not quite the same, is *Guidance Goals*. If you look up *Guidance Goals*, the *Thesaurus* will refer you to *Guidance Objectives* in your search. It will also point out under *Guidance Objectives* that this term is used for (UF) *Guidance Goals*.

In searching, it is sometimes desirable to use a broad term (BT) such as *groups* and at other times to use a narrower term (NT) such as *discussion groups*. This shows a hierarchic relationship between terms. A related term (RT) shows another term that you might want to follow up in order to gain greater understanding of the topic under consideration.

Two other terms may be useful to you. One is *parenthetical qualifiers*. Grades (scholastic) clarify just what kinds of grades are being discussed. Scope notes (SN) limit a particular word to the education usage. The example used in the explanatory material is Acceleration SN–the process of progressing through the school grades at a rate faster than that of

Figure 8 Sample Journal Contents Index/CIJE. The journal contents index is arranged alphabetically by journal title and date. Each article listed is in EJ number sequence. (From *Current Index to Journals in Education*, Level 3, Mock-Up ERIC, page 6.)

the average child. This note eliminates consideration of acceleration in the gravitational sense.

Also included in the *Thesaurus* is a rotated "Descriptor Display." This listing brings related multiword groups together so that you can pick up other terms that might be widely separated in the normal display. Using the display will help you understand how it can aid you in your own work. If you can remember the abbreviations *Use, UF, BT, NT, RT* and *SN*, you can find your way through the *Thesaurus* and use it to advantage.

The ERIC system is more difficult to understand than any of the others you may use. It contains more current data. Already some institutions are providing computer searches that bring up lists of references you can use on a topic. You need to work through the *Thesaurus* if you are to ask the computer the right questions in order to get the data you want without having it buried in a lot of material you cannot use. Learning to use ERIC can be a very important part of your professional education. It will also make your written papers much more acceptable to professors.

EDUCATION INDEX

The *Education Index* has been published by the H. W. Wilson company in New York since 1929. The material emphasizes periodicals but also includes proceedings, yearbooks, bulletins, monographs, and material printed by the United States government. The *Index* is published monthly—except July and August—and is cumulated quarterly and annually, which means that you have to look through the single journals only for three months before moving to a quarterly summary and only three quarters in order to find everything that has been indexed for that year. The early bound volumes cover four-year time spans. The index is organized by both subject and author, although there was a period of about fifteen years when the indexing was by subject only. For each item the title, author, journal, volume, number, date, and pages are listed using abbreviations. The full bibliographic details are given in the front of the volume.

These volumes are a most important place for you to begin your search of the literature, particularly if your topic goes back before the late 1960s. The coverage is broad and comprehensive although not exhaustive. But then, as a beginning researcher, you do not need every last detail for your early papers. The volumes are quite consistent as to the order in which topics appear—new topics are added and others dropped over the years—so you can locate a heading, go back over a number of years, and quickly make a list of the journals you want to consult. Individual papers are listed in more than one place when multiple listing might be helpful. Suggestions are also given for other topics to check. Major headings have subheadings that make searching easier if you know what the limits of your topic are going to be. The flavor of the entries can be gathered from the listings under "Administration," which appeared in a recent issue of the *Index*.

Administration Buildings
Administration of Justice
Administration of Schools
        Bibliography
        City
        Democratic Practices
        District
        Group Plan
        History
        Parent Participation
        Personnel Practices
        Pressure Group Control
        Public Participation
        Research
        State
        Student Participation
        Teacher Participation
        Teaching
        Theories and Principles
        Catholic Schools
        Elementary Schools
        High Schools
        Junior High Schools
        Nursery Schools
        Private Schools
        Rural Schools
        Secondary Schools
        Australia
        California
        Canada
        Great Britain
        Italy
        Maine
        New Jersey
        New York
        Oklahoma
        Oregon

Pennsylvania
Sweden
Venezuela
Administration, Public
Administration, Theory of

Of course, there were one or more articles listed under each subheading. In other issues of the *Index* there would be differences in the states and countries listed depending on which ones were needed to cover the topics in the journals surveyed. By using the subdivisions you could quickly find the names of articles that had dealt with school administration in Sweden during the last forty years. The only real drawback to the *Education Index* compared to some other sources is the lack of annotation; however, you will want to become familiar with this source and be able to use it.

PSYCHOLOGICAL ABSTRACTS

If your topic is related to psychology, learning, growth and development, or similar areas, you will want to become familiar with *Psychological Abstracts*. These abstracts have been published monthly since 1927 by the American Psychological Association, Washington, D.C. Annual indices are published in December covering all the abstracts published during the preceding year. Consolidated indices covering the years 1927-1971 are also available for both authors and subjects.

Journal articles are abstracted, books are annotated, and book chapters written by separate authors are cited. In the journal abstracts the following information is given: abstract number; author(s) and affiliation of the first author only; the title of the article, including any subtitles; the journal in which the article appears with date, volume, and pages; and the abstract. If the abstract refers to previous psychological abstracts, these are listed; if the article is in a foreign language, the English summaries are listed; and if there are more than fifteen references, the number is given. Finally, the source of the abstract is given; usually it has either been written by the original author or has been made by the editors of the abstracts.

Book annotations include the number, the author(s) and the affiliation of the first author. If the book is a compilation, this fact is noted by placing "(Ed(s).)" after the name of the author. The title of the book is followed by the place of publication, the name of the publisher, and the year of publication. The number of pages is shown as xiv (front matter), 555p (volume), followed by the price and a short summary of the contents.

Book chapters are given a citation in very much the same form except that the entries providing author(s) of the chapter, affiliation of the first author, and chapter title are followed by an entry citing the editor of the compilation, which, like any other book, receives a complete citation.

You may find something of what you are seeking by using the subject index or the author index. When you are still trying to find an area to study in depth, you may be helped by skimming the annotations in a general category of entries or even just a subheading of one of the categories. The main headings and principal subheadings in a recent issue were

General
Psychometrics and Statistics
    Test Construction and Validation
    Mathematical Models and Statistics
Perception and Motor Performance
    Perceptual Processes
    Auditory Perception
    Visual Perception
    Motor Processes and Performance
Cognitive Processes and Motivation
    Learning and Thinking and Conditioning
    Attention and Memory
    Motivation and Emotion
Neurology and Physiology
    Neuroanatomy and Electrophysiology
    Physiological Processes
    Genetics

Psychopharmacology and Physiological Intervention
    Brain and Electrical Stimulation and Lesions
    Drug Effects
Animal Psychology
    Learning and Motivation
    Social and Sexual Behavior
    Sensory Processes
Developmental Psychology
    Cognitive and Physical Development
    Emotional and Personality Development
    Social Behavior and Family Relations
    Adult Development and Aging
Cultural Influences and Social Issues
    Culture and Ethnology and Race Relations and Religion
    Social Issues and Social Processes
Social Behavior and Interpersonal Processes
    Group Dynamics and Interpersonal Processes
    Social Perception and Motivation and Attitudes
Communication and Language
Personality
Professional Personnel
Physical and Psychological Disorders
    Mental Disorders
    Behavior Disorders
    Learning Disorders and Mental Retardation
    Speech Disorders
    Physical and Toxic Disorders
Treatment and Prevention
    Psychotherapy and Psychotherapeutic Processes
    Drug Therapy and Drug Rehabilitation
    Behavior and Group Therapy
    Psychoanalysis
    Counseling and Community Mental Health and Crisis
      Intervention
    Physical Treatment
    Social Casework and Rehabilitation
    Hospital Programs and Hospitalization and
      Institutionalization

Educational Psychology
    School Administration and Educational Processes
    Curriculum Development and Teaching Methods
    Academic Learning and Adjustment and Achievement
    Special Education
    Counseling and Measurement
Applied Psychology
    Occupational Guidance and Personnel Selection and
      Training
    Job Performance and Satisfaction
    Management and Leadership
    Organizational Structure and Climate
    Human Factors Engineering and Safety

Some of these topics will seem more related to your interests than will others. Reading the abstracts in areas that seem interesting to you can expand your horizons and show you aspects of the topic that never occurred to you before. Reading the abstracts can also help you to see methods of studying the topic that interests you.

Because searching all of the topics on a subject or even all the abstracts on a simple topic can be very time consuming, the *Psychological Abstracts* provides a computer search service that varies in cost depending on the amount of computer time used, but that generally runs from forty to sixty dollars. Because the steps taken for a computer search can help you make a simpler search of your own, I am listing the information you would have to supply in order to have a search made for you.

1. Descriptors relevant to main topic—list of words or phrases such as
    Early Learning
    Infant Learning
    Infant Conditioning
2. Descriptors limiting the main topic—specific subjects of interest such as
    Disadvantaged
    Female
    First Born

Note: The more restrictive the categories the more expensive the search will be, so do not overdo your restrictions.

3. Search Qualifications

Population: ___ human ___ animal ___ specific animal

Age (approximate): ___ infants ___ child ___ adolescent

___ college ___ adults ___ aged

Publication date: ___ (presently cannot go earlier than 1967.)

4. Sort Requirement

No sort: ___

Author sort: ___ (This runs the price up.)

5. Intended Use

You may find it useful to invest forty or fifty dollars to see what a professional look at the field would be like. You will want to explore some aspects of *Psychological Abstracts* early in your career as a student of education.

CHILD DEVELOPMENT ABSTRACTS AND BIBLIOGRAPHY

A number of other sets of abstracts are important to you as a beginning researcher. The Society for Research in Child Development publishes *Child Development Abstracts and Bibliography,* in which are pulled together articles from medicine, psychology, biology, sociology, and education. The diversity reflects the multidisciplinary backgrounds of the study of child development.

The monthly journal follows the format listed below.

Abstracts of Articles

Each of these gives the author(s) and the affiliation of the first author, the title of the article, the name of the journal, the date, volume and pages on which the article appears, and the abstract, with a credit for the person who wrote the abstract.

The major headings under which the abstracts were grouped in a recent issue follow:

Biology Including Infancy
Clinical Medicine and Public Health
Developmental and Comparative Psychology
Experimental Psychology Including Learning Phenomena
Personality
Sociology and Social Psychology
Education, Educational Psychology and Counseling
Psychiatry, Clinical Psychology and Other Clinical Studies

Book Notices
This section of the journal is the principal part of the bibliography shown in the title of the journal. The book notices include the author(s), the title of the book, the publisher, year of publication, pages, price, and a short annotation of the book.

Books Received
This is the other part of the bibliography. Although these books have been received by the Society for review, they have not been issued for anyone to review and may not be. The listing shows the author, title, publisher, year, pages, and cost.

Author Index for the Journal

Subject Index for the Journal

List of Periodicals Regularly Searched
As you can see from this short outline, there are many kinds of papers that could be helped by skimming the *Child Development Abstracts and Bibliography.* You should become familiar with it.

SOCIOLOGICAL ABSTRACTS

These abstracts are very much the same in form as the *Psychological Abstracts* and the *Child Development Abstracts and Bibliography.* The major users of the *Sociological Abstracts* are sociologists rather than educators, and many parts of the volume are not of much professional interest to the teacher; however, many of you will find articles of interest under these headings:

Social Psychology
Group Interactions
Sociology of Education
The Family and Socialization
Sociology of Knowledge
Feminist Studies

SOCIOLOGY OF EDUCATION ABSTRACTS

An English publication, *Sociology of Education Abstracts,* is used extensively by people interested in educational sociology. Many of the journal articles that are abstracted are American, but about two thirds of them are from other parts of the world.
     The major headings covered in 1974 included

Administration and Organization
Curriculum
Educational Research as an Activity
Goals and Functions of Education
Guidance and Counseling/School Psychology
Historical Development of Education
The Teaching-Learning Process
Tests and Measurements

The principal sociological study areas were

Sociological Analysis
Primary Units of Social Life
Basic Social Institutions

     You can see from the diversity of this list that you should consult these abstracts if you are working in the field of educational sociology.

BUROS MENTAL MEASUREMENT YEARBOOKS

When you start to prepare a paper on tests and measurements, you will want to consult Buros *Mental Measurement Yearbooks* in addition to the items you find in ERIC, the *Education Index,* or *Psychological Abstracts.* Seven of these yearbooks have been published; they come out at somewhat irregular intervals and certainly not annually. Buros has developed them as a labor of love—some might say hate—in order to help improve tests and testing procedures. He claims that more than half the tests reviewed should never have been published. He also says that although one may make such extravagant claims for a test that they cannot be fulfilled by any test, if the test is packaged in an attractive manner, and merchandised energetically, there will be people who will buy it and think that the results are valid. He wants test users to be more sophisticated in their appraisal of tests in the light of their own needs. He suggests extreme skepticism about all tests that do not provide validity and reliability data and clear descriptions of the way the tests were developed. His aims in developing the yearbooks are clearly stated in the introduction to the *Seventh Mental Measurements Yearbook*:

1. To provide information about tests published as separates throughout the English speaking world.
2. To present frankly critical test reviews written by testing and subject specialists representing various viewpoints.
3. To provide extensive bibliographies of verified references on the construction, use, and validity of special tests.
4. To make readily available the critical portions of test reviews appearing in professional journals.
5. To present fairly exhaustive listings of new and revised books on testing along with evaluative excerpts from representative reviews which these books receive in professional journals (Buros 1972, p. xxvii).

The table of contents shown in Table 2 gives an idea of the scope of the coverage, and the page numbers show the intensity of the reviews in a particular field. For instance, Achievement

Table of Contents

VOLUME I

	PAGE
CONTRIBUTING TEST REVIEWERS	xi
PREFACE	xxv
INTRODUCTION	xxvii
TESTS AND REVIEWS	I
ACHIEVEMENT BATTERIES	I
CHARACTER AND PERSONALITY	68
Nonprojective	68
Projective	390
ENGLISH	465
Literature	502
Spelling	510
Vocabulary	514
FINE ARTS	521
Art	521
Music	522
FOREIGN LANGUAGES	536
Arabic	547
Chinese	547

	PAGE
English	548
French	553
German	575
Greek	582
Hebrew	583
Italian	583
Latin	588
Russian	589
Spanish	591
INTELLIGENCE	606
Group	606
Individual	727
Specific	809
MATHEMATICS	842
Algebra	890
Arithmetic	911
Calculus	924
Geometry	926
Trigonometry	933

VOLUME II

	PAGE
TESTS AND REVIEWS (CONTINUED)	
MISCELLANEOUS	937
Blind	938
Business Education	938
Courtship and Marriage	950
Driving and Safety Education	960
Education	962
Health and Physical Education	974
Home Economics	984

	PAGE
Industrial Arts	986
Listening Comprehension	992
Philosophy	995
Psychology	996
Religious Education	996
Scoring Machines and Services	997
Socioeconomic Status	1007
Test Programs	1009
MULTI-APTITUDE BATTERIES	1046

	PAGE
READING	1068
Diagnostic	1109
Miscellaneous	1132
Oral	1146
Readiness	1148
Special Fields	1194
Study Skills	1201
SCIENCE	1215
Biology	1245
Chemistry	1251
Geology	1262
Physics	1262
SENSORY-MOTOR	1266
SOCIAL STUDIES	1295
Economics	1303
Geography	1308
History	1310
Political Science	1319
Sociology	1324
SPEECH AND HEARING	1325
Hearing	1325
Speech	1336
VOCATIONS	1370
Clerical	1388
Interests	1395

	PAGE
Manual Dexterity	1481
Mechanical Ability	1483
Miscellaneous	1488
Selection and Rating Forms	1496
Specific Vocations	1497
Accounting	1497
Business	1498
Computer Programming	1501
Dentistry	1505
Engineering	1506
Law	1507
Medicine	1509
Miscellaneous	1514
Nursing	1517
Selling	1519
Skilled Trades	1520
Supervision	1524
Transportation	1532
BOOKS AND REVIEWS	1533
PERIODICAL DIRECTORY AND INDEX	1847
PUBLISHERS DIRECTORY AND INDEX	1853
INDEX OF BOOK TITLES	1862
INDEX OF TEST TITLES	1871
INDEX OF NAMES	1895
CLASSIFIED INDEX OF TESTS	1968

TABLE 2 Table of Contents, The Seventh Mental Measurements Yearbook (Oscar K. Buros, *The Seventh Mental Measurements Yearbook*, Highland Park, N. J.: The Gryphon Press, 1972, pp. ix-x. By permission of the author and publisher.)

Batteries run from page 1-67. You will find these yearbooks very important in your study of measurement.

PREPARING A BIBLIOGRAPHY

The card catalog and the various indices and abstracts including ERIC provide you with the information you need to construct the basic bibliography for your reading and writing. Once you have limited the topic and refined it somewhat, you will be able to determine, at least in general, whether a particular book or document will be useful to you as you read in depth. The practice of recording the potential sources on cards to summarize contents of the readings helps you systematize your reading and note gathering. If you copy the complete reference as you search through the library resources, you will form habits that will be useful to you for the rest of your academic life. Many of the sources will turn out to be irrelevant or unnecessary and you will not use the card in writing this particular paper, but you can keep it for possible use another time. Once you have the cards constructed, the abstracts can help you gather pertinent data quickly. The microfiches from RIE contain the complete document, and you will want to go from the abstracts to the whole article when the abstract looks as though the article will be important in the study you are conducting. Often, going to the whole article requires consulting the listed journals. Even the articles that you read that do not fit into your present topic are likely to contain information that is useful to you in broadening your own general knowledge.

Papers in Specific Fields

Chapter 1 gives a brief overview of different major areas into which the professional field of education is often divided. The decision about how to categorize the subdivisions was based on common course titles. Many other groupings are made in colleges and universities, but there is usually a way in which you can figure out that Psychological Foundations of Education—to take one example—includes what we have listed as Educational Psychology, Child Growth and Development, and Tests and Measurements. Your text's table of contents will give you an indication of what is covered. Courses like Introduction to Education usually survey a broad spectrum of material that other courses cover in greater detail. You can use the ideas and suggested approaches as they best fit your own situation.

This section has been divided into topics, but there is a great deal of overlap between them. Is social psychology, sociology or psychology? Surveys are used in many areas besides sociology, although they are probably more common in that discipline than in most others. Read all of these topics and choose ideas and techniques from any of them that fit your purpose rather than restrict yourself to the section labeled to match your course. The different labels will give you a generalized framework that puts the many little pieces together into a whole that you can refer to as you continue your studies.

PHILOSOPHY OF EDUCATION

As mentioned in chapter 1, many of the topics that are the concern of the philosophy of education are once again becoming live issues after a period during which nearly everyone believed that the questions had been answered definitively. Sooner or later you will face questions that fall into this category, if you have not already done so. Who should be educated? "Everyone," of course, has been the answer; but we have not included the severely mentally retarded, those in mental hospitals, those in jails, and, all too often, the migrant workers' children and others who do not fit comfortably into standard life-styles. Many teachers are raising questions about whether young people of the high school group who are resisting the learning being offered should be kept in school. A related question concerns the nature of the education that should be offered. Should it be the same for all? If not, are you discriminating against anyone unfairly? If you do offer the same education, are you discriminating against those who really need a different kind of education?

Who should pay for education? Should the elderly retired who are on small pensions have to support lavish schools? Should those who are keeping the population down by not having children be required to support schools for the children of less enlightened citizens? Should people who send their children to private, parochial, or free schools have to support their own chosen schools and the public schools for other children as well? Voucher systems, which allow parents to designate the school to which their child will go with the tax support for that child also going to the school, are designed to answer this question in one way. Is this answer for the public good?

What moral and ethical principles should be taught? Who should decide? Should schools teach nationalism? Patriotism? Is patriotism ours and good and the same ideas from a different context nationalism and bad? Should schools teach reverence for capitalism? Socialism? Communism? Who should decide? The strongest? The loudest?

Should bilingualism be encouraged and supported in the Southwest? New York? Florida? Maine? Minnesota? Should schools teach dialects? Black? South Carolinian? Bostonian? Who should decide? On what basis?

Schools have changed more in the last decade than in all the preceding fifty years. Many of the changes have been made on a case by case basis without referring them to any major principles. In spite of the fact that these philosophical topics are of vital importance to the future of the schools, none of the major sources listed in chapter 3 has a principal heading called Philosophy of Education, although many of the topics mentioned under philosophy show up in various ways in different places in the indices.

When you start a paper in the area of educational philosophy, you need to be a skeptic and ask "Why?" at every turn. This question should be supplemented by "How do you know?" Even the apparently self-evident truths such as "Universal education is good," need to be questioned and thought about. Much of your research will require going back to sources that are old if you are going to understand the roots and significance of the arguments. Papers in the area of philosophy are almost pure library research. When you have finished the paper, some of your prejudices will have been confirmed by supporting knowledge even though your opinions may not have changed at all. On the other hand, you may find evidence that runs counter to your prejudice. Sometimes you will reject the evidence, but hopefully sometimes you will revise your prejudice.

HISTORY OF EDUCATION

In writing on this topic, you might find it worthwhile to consult the *Research Guide in History*, part of this series written by John R. M. Wilson (1974). A specialized topic within cultural and social history, the history of education goes back to ancient times. It is surprising and exciting to come across items three thousand years old that could have been duplicated in the local school within the last month. For example, a letter from a boy in Egypt to his absent father in Cairo requested him to bring a certain toy when he returned. In the letter the boy promised to lie on the floor and scream and kick if the father returned without the toy (about 1500 B. C.). Teachers are still dealing with children who have learned to use tantrums to get their own way. Also Euclid's *Elements* was still the basic text in geometry in 1910 although it was written about 300 B. C. The same problems that are of concern to the philosophers of education appear in historical annals, and frequently the two disciplines propose similar solutions to similar problems.

A cycle of about twenty to thirty years seems to be sufficient to give an older person the feeling that he or she has been here before. By looking back, it is possible to find that the new solutions are not really new and often do not even use different words to present the same ideas. Although sometimes the ideas disappear for a time because of accidents of history, many are found not to be as bright with promise as they once seemed. You can save yourself a lot of wear and tear if you can recognize which ideas are good and which seem to be attractive but are fundamentally unsound.

A paper on the history of education will be based almost entirely on library research. You will want to consult two sets of abstracts after you have looked over the references in your text. *America: History and Life: A Guide to Periodical Literature* (Boehm, 1964) is a quarterly publication that covers articles on United States and Canadian history. The section on social and cultural history is most likely to provide articles on the history of education. The 150-word abstract will give you an idea as to whether you want to follow up a particular reference in the complete, fully referenced article. *Historical Abstracts, 1775-1945: Bibliography of the World's Periodical Literature* (Boehm, 1955) is a quarterly that covers the world in much the same way that *America: History and Life* covers the United States and Canada. Many of the roots of American education lie in things that happened in Europe; thus new light on the history of European countries often can be helpful in understanding what has happened locally.

When you study historical topics in order to prepare a paper, there are a number of things you should remember.

1. Most points that are worth studying have been and sometimes still are controversial. Under the circumstances you should get both sides of the controversy and document them in your paper. It is usually easier to get documentation for the side that won because it proved to be the most popular. You have heard, for instance, that support of parochial schools by the taxing agencies is illegal because it violates the principle of separation of church and state. If you were going to study this topic seriously, you would want to know the basis on which the church and state were separated—they are *not* in many countries. In addition to this basic point, you would want to pursue the reasons for the close identification of parochial schools with the churches they represent. You might want to deepen your argument by following the same controversy in Canadian history where, except in British Columbia, the practice as regards tax support of parochial education is the opposite to that in the United States. Since the basic cultures in Canada and the United States are very similar, why did school financing develop differently? An enormous amount of data is available on the separation side of this argument. Much less is available on the state support of both parochial and public schools, and it is harder for you to locate.

2. The winning side may not have been *right*. Along with most Americans, I happen to believe in the separation of the church and state. On pragmatic grounds, I believe in a single publicly supported school system, but this does not mean that the argument for the other side may not be sounder or that a different way of financing education might not be better for the country. Your job as a historian of education is to understand both sides of an issue and to reevaluate the evidence.

3. Evaluate your sources. This admonition is difficult to follow in the light of the two points listed above. The dominant viewpoint became dominant because it was originally and has since had the support of the most prestigious people in the discipline. The other side has been supported by losers, which often makes their evidence suspect. As a beginner in the field, you cannot prove an expert wrong, but you can look at both arguments to see whether a side won because of greater power or because of greater logic.

An original study of a local school can result in a history paper that would be exciting both for you and for your professor. To write such a paper, you would want to explore a particular aspect of the history. You might investigate the problems involved in financing and constructing the buildings, or the selection of the principals or vice-principals over the years and their impact on the school. Perhaps you might trace the changes in methods used to teach reading and compare the results, or study the development of vocational education provisions over the years. There are many different topics that will help you see your own place in the scheme of things and that can be researched by using the minutes of the Board of Education, the local newspaper files, the school newspaper files, and the memories of some of the older active or retired teachers.

Whatever your topic, if you do original work using primary sources, you will become, at least to a limited extent, a historian rather than just a paper writer. History can come very much alive as you delve into it. Looking for roots to old debates can clarify present problems for you. Close study will take a great deal of time, but the time will be well spent.

EDUCATIONAL SOCIOLOGY

Considerations of sociological import are having more of an impact on what happens in schools than are ideas from any other field of study. Most of the federal aid to education goes to schools for the express purpose of increasing the opportunities of the lower social classes. Decisions about busing and school integration depend on sociological studies. The classroom is studied as a social situation whose dynamics enhance the self-concept of some pupils and lower the self-concept of others. Evaluation of teachers by pupils reflects the idea that group processes can be critically important in the efficient performance of teaching duties. Decisions about whether to group pupils into classes along homogeneous or heterogeneous lines reflect sociological pressures. Putting policemen into the hallways of schools in order to protect both pupils and teachers from violence has sociological implications. As you can see, many of the conditions that will affect your life as a teacher are determined by sociological considerations. Writing a paper in this area of educational study may be primarily a library experience, or it may involve you in actually making a small study in the field.

When you are writing a paper in the area of educational sociology, all the resources such as ERIC, the *Education Index, Psychological Abstracts, Child Growth Abstracts, Sociology of Education Abstracts*, as well as *Sociological Abstracts*, will be of value to you. Many of the same articles are indexed and abstracted in the different indices. You will, however, have to become alert in deciding which articles are based on hard research data and which merely express opinion that has been inferred from research data that does not support it.

For instance, Coleman et al. (1966) found that children from schools in lower socioeconomic districts did better in their school work if they moved to schools that were predominantly middle class. If this improvement were to take place, it was necessary for the school to continue to be essentially a middle-class school. The effect of the inclusion of the disadvantaged on the performance of the middle-class youngsters, when the complexion of the school remained middle class, was either neutral or advantageous. If the complexion of the school changed to become essentially a lower-class school, the advantage for the transported children disappeared, and the middle-class children suffered as well. Much of the busing controversy has grown out of this research, although practically no one on either side has looked at the study critically. "Lower class" has been translated to mean black or Chicano, and "middle class" has been translated to mean Anglo. No attention has been paid to economic conditions and proportions that determine the class character of a school. As a result a situation arises, as happened in Boston, where children are bused from a poor black school to a poor white school in the hope that busing would improve the educational prospects of the bused children. But Coleman's research makes any such improvement seem unlikely.

Torrance and Arsan (1963) found homogeneous groups more effective than heterogeneous groups in productivity, self-concept, and liking for the task. The advantages were greatest for the lower IQ children. Since this research was done, homogeneous grouping in school has been practically eliminated because it was thought to discriminate against the less able students. The support for the discriminatory viewpoint has centered on *Pygmalion in the Classroom*, a research study by Rosenthal and Jacobson (1968). The essence of this research was that if teachers thought a student could or would do better, the work of that student improved dramatically. Robert L. Thorndike (1968) analyzed Rosenthal and Jacobson's findings and compared the research study to a clock striking fourteen. Thorndike did not say that belief in children's ability would not lead to improved performance, but he did say Rosenthal and Jacobson's data was unbelievable.

The sociological impact of certain studies and the misinterpretation that springs from them have been mentioned only because there are many active political decisions being made that are based on subtle shifts in the evidence. You can trace almost any current sociological problem back to basic research of one kind or another and compare the application with the research findings. This kind of tracing makes an excellent paper from whose preparation you will learn about many facets of our society.

You have probably already found that much sociological research involves large groups of students, teachers, counselors or administrators, and complex statistical treatments of results in order to determine the significance of any differences that have been found. This kind of research is usually beyond the beginner in the field although you might have an opportunity to participate in such studies by helping to gather or tabulate the data. However, there are small sociological studies you can make that will get you started as a researcher and will give you a feel for collecting and interpreting data.

The Sociogram and Group Dynamics

It is possible that you could administer a sociogram in which you ask students to name the three students they would like to have as members of a committee to decorate for a party, to work on a joint paper for a grade, or to go for a weekend to a camp. You will probably find that there are differences in who is chosen for different kinds of activities. Occasionally you can ask for the person or persons who would definitely not be acceptable, but this question has some dangers. Sociograms such as these can be administered in a variety of schools or classes with different socioeconomic backgrounds to help you see whether patterns are the same across groups although different for choices. This kind of study allows you to examine the dynamics of the group.

Interaction Analysis

Another study you can make is based on a classroom interaction analysis such as that developed by Flanders (1962), in which you systematically record the kind of interaction between the teacher and one or more pupils. Since you should have such an analysis made on your own interaction with pupils as you are student teaching, it is helpful to go through the process with an experienced teacher. Differential studies can be made recording the interaction of the teacher with pupils of different socioeconomic levels, different intellectual levels, or different social adjustment. A simple comparison of the means of positive and negative interactions can make a respectable study.

Questionnaires, Surveys, and Attitude Scales

You can use questionnaires, surveys, or attitude scales to test hypotheses about differences in group perceptions. These instruments are harder to devise properly than they appear to be, but making one and having it criticized by your professor can provide a very good lesson about the possibility of biasing results. Selecting the sample to be surveyed can also be more difficult than it looks, but you can learn a great deal by reading about sampling, stratified sampling, and randomized sampling, and then selecting your own sample.

Data on many important topics are collected by means of surveys, questionnaires, and attitude scales. Attitudes about reading, self-concept as a person, vocational goals, attitudes toward premarital sex or involvement in the drug scene are only a few of these topics. The big problem in this kind of survey, one that plagues even the work of the professional pollsters who run the Gallup poll, is structuring the questions so that you get the subject's own idea rather than what the person thinks you want him or her to say.

If you do a study for your paper you will, of course, have to do some library research in order to define your techniques, to see what has already been done, and to devise a topic that is manageable in the time and space you have. You will be learning many things that are valuable, including skills in research techniques. Perhaps more important, you will be developing an awareness of the pitfalls of research that will help you to read more critically and perceptively.

ECONOMICS OF EDUCATION

You are less likely to be asked to write a paper in the economics of education than in other social science fields. However, this is a field that will affect each of you very closely. Your salary, the buildings in which you teach, and the supplies you have to work with are all dependent on economic factors. Topics listed in ERIC under "Finance" and "Facilities" are loaded with economic implications. You can make library studies of the trade-off between spending money for salaries and for other educational uses. A bond for a million dollars paid off over 25 years at 6 percent interest costs the same as do six teachers at annual salaries of $12,886 for the same 25 years. You might find it worth your while to make some studies of other financial matters, such as the relative cost of teacher aides compared to teachers, which would give you perspective on the choice between reducing class size and having help in a larger class group for the same money.

Of course there are many other kinds of economic studies. One might determine the cost of teaching an average seventh grade pupil to play volleyball or consider the average gain in academic performance attributable to the cost of busing students from one school to another. This latter study would be beyond your capability as a beginning researcher, but it might help you simply to realize that studies can be made of the cost effectiveness of different school programs. You may want to make such studies for yourself when you are asked to support bond issues; innovations such as busing students for racial balance; or payment of coaches, drama teachers, or band leaders with an extra period free or with more money. You will undoubtedly uncover some amazing facts.

GROWTH AND DEVELOPMENT

In many institutions professors require students who are enrolled in growth and development classes to make observations of, and write reports on, children or adolescents in live settings. Often the nature of the observations and the form of the report are detailed very clearly, and as a student you will have no trouble following the plan provided. Despite the fact that a great many students have made mini-studies of this nature, basic research in child growth and development is among the most difficult and time consuming. The Berkeley Growth Studies trace individual changes in intellectual scores over a period of thirty-six years (Bayley, 1970). The Gesell studies at Yale extend over a similar period. These are longitudinal studies in which individual children were studied as they developed into adults over a period of many years. Cross-sectional studies in which groups of children of different ages are examined are more common. Each kind of research has difficulties peculiar to it. Although there is regularity to the pattern of development, there is quite a lot of variability among individual children of the same age. In cross-sectional studies, unless the groups are large, changes can be obscured by the selection process. In longitudinal studies, children are likely to move to another part of the country, and by repeatedly using the same measuring instrument, such as the Binet intelligence test, one can introduce practice effects. But in spite of the difficulties inherent in major research projects, you will find the experience of carrying out small studies both surprising and rewarding.

The main library reference source will be *Child Development Abstracts and Bibliography* although ERIC, *Psychological Abstracts* in the section on Developmental Psychology, and the *Education Index* all have titles and abstracts that can be helpful in getting you started. You should do considerable reading before you start a formal field study; otherwise you may think you are mistaken in what you discover. Of course, some informal observing along with the reading will give you a better start than would all reading or all field work. Some important concepts, such as those developed by Fantz on very early perception in infants or the investigation of critical developmental periods by Burton L. White, can be mastered only through library research. But many field studies can be done in rather brief periods. A few of these will be suggested in the following section.

Jean Piaget

The work of Jean Piaget provides many small studies that can be carried out easily by a newcomer to experimentation, even though it takes much practice and training to be an expert in the Piagetan method of child study. You may, for example, test the ability of children to conserve volume. In such an experiment children may see that the volumes in two similar containers are equal; but if they are quite young, they will feel sure that when they have poured one into a container that differs in shape the volume has changed. In a similar experiment with mass, using clay balls that are rolled into sausage shapes or flattened, young children will be sure that the mass has changed along with the shape even though slightly older children will not believe anyone could be so dumb. Another Piagetan experiment you might try involves asking children of different ages to rank sticks in order from largest to smallest and then to draw the arrangement from memory. You will find that the way children go at this task varies dramatically as they change in age from two and a half to six years old. In quite a different kind of study you can ask children about dreams and where the dreams are. Some of the children will say dreams are in the room; others will say in the head. The answers change with age changes. Piaget has spent fifty years doing different kinds of probing to see how children of different ages think. You can reconstruct many of his experiments, and doing so will help you see children in a different light.

Arnold Gesell

In his books *The First Five Years of Life, The Child from Five to Ten,* and *Youth: The Years from Ten to Sixteen,* Gesell (1940, 1946, 1956) provides tasks that you can use to see where particular children are on his developmental scale. For instance, you can check two-year-old children to see if they can run using heel and toe steps rather than taking flat-footed steps. You may note how they kick a ball. Are they able to identify objects in a picture? Can they dress and undress themselves? Do they talk to other children almost as though talking to themselves? If you are going to do a paper on this kind of observation, you should work directly from the test activities outlined in the appropriate volume.

Of course the ideas listed here are only the barest kind of beginning to the topics you can explore and the techniques you can use, but I hope these examples will stimulate you to go out and study children and young people with perception and affection.

EDUCATIONAL PSYCHOLOGY

More research papers are written in educational psychology than in any other education field. Much of the research, such as that on a comparison of the genetic and the environmental factors in intelligence, is very controversial, and much of the rest of it is, according to practical school people, almost useless. Since educational psychology is my own area of specialization, I think that research on how people learn is crucial if a professional teacher is to understand what is going on in the minds of the students. This, of course, is a personal bias. All of the major library indices list articles that you ought to study if you are doing an educational psychology paper. The *Child Development Abstracts and Bibliography* and the *Sociological Abstracts* cover many articles on learning, learning disabilities, intelligence, behavioral objectives, and other topics that fall within the confines of educational psychology.

As you read reports of old research, you may spot points at which a study is faulty. These insights often come to intelligent students who do not know the field very well, students who have not yet learned that certain findings are accepted by everyone, hence must be true! A case in point is the repeal of *Thorndike's Law of Exercise* (that practice strengthened learning bonds and disuse weakened learning bonds) defined in 1913 by E. L. Thorndike. Trowbridge and Cason (1932) did an experiment in which they had blindfolded students draw a line three inches long without telling them of their success or failure. The students did not improve their drawing until they were told of their successes and failures. This study was accepted by Thorndike and by almost everyone else as proof that exercise without the intervention of the *Law of Effect* (that learning accompanied by satisfying feeling strengthened learning bonds and learning accompanied by annoyance weakened learning bonds) was useless. It has very recently occurred to me that as the experiment was set up, the students were not practicing drawing a line three inches long. They were practicing drawing lines blindfolded. Their lines could have been drawn more efficiently, but as the experiment was set up it contained a nonsequitur. This discovery does not render the *Law of Exercise* invalid, but it does mean that some other experiments should be done. The possibility that you might find such a flaw ought to encourage you to read not with complacent acceptance of what is written, but critically, always seeking an opportunity to improve the state of our understanding.

In areas such as the nature and nurture of intelligence, you will write your paper on the basis of library research. Indeed, in the study of most theories as theories, you will use the library very extensively; but these are many areas in which you can do small experiments that will help you to make someone else's study better controlled and more acceptable.

Operant Conditioning Experiments

Operant conditioning is the easiest and quickest way of changing undesirable behavior in another person. It is a technique that has many important uses in the classroom, from alleviating behavior problems to helping students learn content materials. The first step is to identify the behavior that you do not like and wish to change. The subject of operant conditioning can be a student, a roommate, a husband, a wife, or even a dog.

Establishing baselines is the beginning of the treatment. You count the number of times that the subject behaves in the offending manner during a given period of time—half an hour, half a day, or any period you fix. Record what you were doing immediately before, during, and after the undesired behavior took place. You need these two bits of information in order to see whether there really has been a change and to decide how you were contributing to the undesired activity.

Conditioning proper begins as you select a reinforcement such as a smile, a word of praise, a hug, or a piece of candy that the subject of the conditioning really likes. Use the reinforcement each time the conditionee moves toward doing the right rather than the wrong thing. For instance, if swearing bothers you, give a reinforcement each time the conditionee speaks without swearing. Make the reinforcement come *immediately* after the desired response and before the undesired response might occur. It will take a bit of practice to find the correct timing and to make the reinforcement seem natural. Continue conditioning by lengthening the time between reinforcements while still discouraging the undesired activity.

Determine new performance levels by repeating the count for the undesired activity during the same time span used for the baselines. If you have been really successful, the count will be zero, but you may be satisfied if an improvement of 90 percent is achieved. Should you have been less than 100 percent successful, note your own activities before, during, and immediately after the undesired activity. They will probably have changed also since you will be reinforcing rather than criticizing, an activity often causally related to the original problem.

Testing the conditioning can be accomplished by stopping the reinforcements and going back to the kind of activity that was associated with the undesired activity before the experiment started. You may want to skip this part of the experiment. You can draw a graph to show the difference between the behavior at the beginning and at the end of the experiment. In your write-up, describe your goals—the desired behavior—the undesired activity, the method of establishing the baselines, the nature of the reinforcements, the methods of their application, the final count of the successful end of the experiment, and your interpretation of why the conditioning turned out as it did.

One important aspect of operant conditioning is that the process emphasizes giving rewards for doing the right thing rather than punishments for doing the wrong. This way of acting is pleasanter for you and for the person whose behavior you are trying to change. Once you have mastered them, you will probably use these techniques as a regular part of your life style.

Classical Conditioning Experiments

In classical conditioning, one stimulus is substituted for another that originally prompted a desired activity. Classical conditioning is not nearly as useful in the classroom as is operant conditioning. Indeed, there is argument that classical conditioning is just a special case of operant conditioning. However, you can easily set up a simple experiment that will demonstrate successful conditioning.

Suppose that you have the task of getting dinner for yourself and your roommate. You can condition your roommate to come for dinner on a signal other than calling. The signal can be anything you choose to make it. If you select a particular record as the signal, make a regular practice of starting the record immediately before calling that dinner is ready. Quite soon you will not need to call that dinner is ready. The record will act as a signal.

When you write up this experiment, describe the situation. Tell what signal you used, and report the number of pairings needed for partial conditioning and the number needed to get complete conditioning. There are many similar experiments in which one stimulus is substituted for another. You can have fun thinking up one of your own.

The Use of Affects

Affects are either pleasure stimulating or punishment stimulating. Pleasure-producing affects lead to repetition and continuation of the activities with which they are associated. Punishment-producing ones increased avoidance activity, which may lead to different responses, which may be either desirable or undesirable from your point of view. An excellent paper can be built on the experimental determination of which activities on your part will lead to pleasure affects for particular students and which will lead to punishment affects. It may surprise you that different students respond differently to the same kinds of overt activity. Skill in determining whether or not a particular planned reinforcer—pleasure producer—is actually reinforcing is essential to using operant conditioning successfully. In writing up your experiment you should describe the students, the tentative reinforcers, and the outcomes in behavior as far as the students are concerned. Do not group this kind of data except to summarize by saying that activity A was reinforcing for x students and apparently punishing for y students.

Writing Behavioral Objectives

Ordinarily, writing behavioral objectives is a part of a larger activity such as teaching a unit of subject matter; however, this task is sufficiently important that you should have some practice in setting up your objectives. There are five parts to a well-written set of objectives.

1. Describe the exact nature of the learning task.
2. Designate the learner—for example, a third grade pupil or a student in first year algebra.
3. Use an action verb such as "to count," "to define," or "to write" to indicate what is done.
4. Give the outcome or the product of the instruction.
5. Give the standard that will be considered an acceptable level of performance.

You can see that you could write behavioral objectives for either the operant conditioning or the classical conditioning exercises that were listed earlier. There has been criticism of written behavioral objectives because it is easier to write them for rote kinds of learning. It is possible, but harder, to write behavioral objectives for conceptualizations or for creative self-directing activities. Ways of doing just that are set out in one of our books, *Psychological Foundations of Learning and Teaching* (Wilson, Robeck, and Michael, 1974).

Mastery Learning Papers

A great deal of interest has been developing in setting up schools on the basis that students will master a certain body of content rather than that they will pass. Inherent in the idea is that some students will move more quickly and others more slowly over the same materials, but all will come to the skill now demonstrated by those who get "A" grades. Well-developed behavioral objectives that specify individual success make mastery learning an easier goal to attain. You might write a paper on this topic, describing how you could define and reach the goal of mastery learning for all of your pupils. It would be even more impressive to describe the goal and then to carry it out with a class group. In order for you to do that, you would have to have access to a class and freedom to restructure it on the mastery learning paradigm.

There are many other areas in educational psychology in which you can do experiments and write papers, but perhaps these samples are enough to get you started. Again, the purpose of teaching is to get learning to take place. If you define what you are doing or trying to do and then measure the degree of your success, you can improve your competence as a teacher.

MEASUREMENT AND EVALUATION

Papers on this subject usually belong to one of two broad categories—sample tests of your own devising, or evaluations of standardized tests. You may want to use a particular kind of test as a part of a larger study, and to do so you will need to decide which test would be appropriate. Inevitably, as part of your student teaching, you will have to prepare and administer tests whether or not they are part of a course requirement.

Your Own Tests

Considering the critical decisions that are based on the results of teacher-made tests and examinations, such as the failure or promotion of students, their entry into a university or into a vocational training program, tests should be better than they are. You will want to search the literature on ways of writing good examinations, but a few principles might help you to cover certain topics if you are preparing a paper to demonstrate the effectiveness of your test.

You should do your best to insure that you have approached *content validity*, that is, that the test gives reasonable weight to each of the objectives of the course. Content validity can best be achieved by setting up a two-way grid with the content topics along one dimension and skill processes or thought level along another. Bloom's *Taxonomy of Educational Objectives* (Bloom et al., 1956), in which he described skills of comprehension, application, analysis, synthesis, and evaluation, is an example of one set of process objectives. Questions should be devised to sample both content and process over the whole range of the specified objectives. Most teacher-made examinations violate this principle and pick an inordinate number of questions from either one topic or one process level. It is easier to make up questions on some topics than others, but if you can demonstrate content validity your paper will be superior from its inception.

Your test should also have *predictive validity*. Usually tests are given to determine whether or not a student can go on to further work of one kind or another. If you can show that your questions really separate those who can do the next level of work from those who cannot, yours will be a good test.

Your test should have *reliability*. This means that you should get the same grade when you score it before dinner that you do when you score it after a good meal. The type of test you design, whether objective or essay, has a bearing on the reliability. Generally, objective tests are more reliable than essay tests; however, they may not measure as well such parameters as the student's ability to explain his or her ideas. Objective questions can be made more reliable in a number of ways. Some of these are described in Chapter 18 of *Psychological Foundations of Learning and Teaching* (Wilson, Robeck, and Michael, 1974). Practice in writing good questions, in sampling the breadth and width of the field, and in tying the success of the test to the competence necessary for the next ability level can make you a superior test writer. Your paper will be the stronger for having attended to these important aspects of test design.

Standardized Tests

If you are asked to evaluate any test, you will want to start by reading the manual and taking the test yourself. There are problems in administering a test to yourself, but by the same token, you will learn many of the pitfalls in the instructions in a way that cannot be duplicated. After your own experience with the test, you might very well administer it to one student, score it, and then attempt to interpret the results to the person to whom you gave the test; however, you must make sure the subject knows that the results may be inaccurate and the interpretation tentative. Having done all of this, you should read what is written about this test in *The Seventh Mental Measurements Yearbook* (Buros, 1972). It is desirable to have had some personal experience with a test before reading these reviews of it.

In writing a report on the test you should include the bibliographic data—the test name, author, publisher, date, and price—as well as other information about the reliability reported by the test maker, the validity and how it was determined, the standardization, including the ability levels, ethnic distributions, and age ranges of students, the size, and the geographic distribution of the subjects in the sample to judge the basis for claims that the sample is representative of the population in general. You will also want to include the time it takes to administer the test and a subjective statement about how favorably the students will respond to the test on the basis of your own experience with it.

You could be asked to develop a set of tests that cover intelligence, personality, interest, special ability, and reading achievement for a particular group. This kind of assignment requires evaluating different tests in each group and putting them all together on some basis. A typical difficulty is that the standardization groups are different for the different tests. You may be asked to make a statistical analysis of the administration of a particular test to some class group. This analysis can be as simple as finding the mean, standard deviation, and perhaps the standard score for different pupils, or it can be much more complicated, requiring analyses of variance, regression equations, or factorial analyses of results. These techniques are beyond most beginning students.

You will need to use tests and measurements all of your teaching life. Because many of your pupils will be evaluated on their success with these materials, you need to understand standardized test scores. Therefore, even if you are not assigned tasks such as those listed in this section, you probably should work them out for your own satisfaction.

COUNSELING AND GUIDANCE

All teachers counsel and guide students in many ways, but not all of them are asked to write papers on topics in the counseling and guidance field of education. Actually there are many subsections of this field. Some areas, such as psychometry, are concerned almost exclusively with testing, in particular with individualized testing. This type of test requires quite specific reports on the way the student has responded as well as an interpretation of the raw scores for this particular pupil.

Papers may stress vocational counseling interviews with different students. In these, the different instruments used to help the students view their own interests, their personalities, and their special aptitudes would need to be displayed along with the kinds of occupations that might be open and suitable for people with these talents and interests. Finally, you might discuss the interaction between the student and the information, and you might describe the steps taken to place the student vocationally or academically.

In personal counseling, papers may be much more related to a running record of the steps taken by the clients to work through their problems. Such steps may be psychotherapeutic in nature, or they may be more behaviorally oriented. In any case, a record needs to be kept by the beginning counselor that will allow his or her supervisor to suggest ways of increasing counseling effectiveness.

In educational counseling, one should record attempts to improve academic functioning, and should report conclusions reached jointly with the client about steps to be taken and about followup to determine the outcome of counseling. Many papers on this kind of counseling will be heavily weighted with interpretations gleaned from sessions recorded either on video or audio tape.

On the other hand, many counseling papers will be research reports dealing with operant conditioning exercises developed to change undesirable behavior of some kind. These papers will provide baselines, treatment descriptions, and evaluations of outcomes. You will normally receive quite specific instructions about how the reports in counseling and guidance are to be made.

In library research there are many sources that bear on one facet or another of counseling and guidance. The following descriptor groups in the *Current Index to Journals in Education*—part of the ERIC system—would need to be examined (see list of descriptor groups on pages 38-42):

010 Abilities
040 Attitudes
060 Behavior
080 Communication
090 Counseling
150 Employment
180 Evaluation
190 Evaluation Techniques
240 Handicapped
250 Health and Safety
350 Occupations
360 Opportunities
370 Organizations (Groups)
380 Personnel and Groups
410 Programs
420 Psychology
430 Race Relations
490 Sociology
500 Standards
520 Tests

This is a much larger number of headings than is discussed in this chapter, but counseling and guidance has many facets.

CURRICULUM AND METHODS

The most common paper requirement in this area is a lesson plan. You may be asked to prepare plans for a term, for a unit of instruction, and for each daily lesson you teach. A shift is taking place in the way in which these plans are being written, with more attention being given to behavioral objectives and to measurement of success in reaching the objectives. Obviously, as far as the content is concerned, it makes a difference whether you are preparing for a kindergarten morning or for a class in advanced algebra. There are, however, general principles that apply to all areas and all subject matters. One of these is that you should know what you are trying to do before you get to class; in other words, you should have a lesson plan. The need for such a plan will be with you all of your teaching life. After you have become experienced you will not need to spend as much time putting things down on paper as you do now, but you will be happier and your students will learn more if you continue to state in quite precise terms what you are trying to accomplish.

Establishing Baselines

One of the hardest parts of preparing to teach any group, from prekindergarten to high school, is to determine what each of the students already knows about the content, skills, or attitudes that are being taught. An enormous amount of teacher effort is wasted teaching children and adolescents things that they already know. Increases in your productivity, an important point with the people who pay the bills, will more easily be made by eliminating unnecessary instruction than by any other means. Children frequently enter first grade already able to read, but the teacher, unaware of this skill, spends an enormous amount of effort teaching them processes they have already mastered. Some students enter eleventh grade American history classes having learned the course material in a similar eighth grade course. The problem is that in the past too often the teacher has taught a lesson for a mythical group of "average" students instead of for individuals. It is necessary for you to discover what individuals know already and to teach them to go on from there. It is much easier to tell you that you should establish baselines and teach individuals than it is to discover these needs and devise strategies for meeting all the different needs in a class. One of the possible ways is to use behavioral objectives to set up mastery learning modules that can be met on an individual basis.

Behavioral Objectives

If you have established your behavioral objectives so that they are well defined and have established ways of measuring the achievement of the objectives by individual pupils, you can use the tests at the beginning of the course to establish your baselines. You will probably write better behavioral objectives for your long-term plans if you use tests to assess beginning competence. Your objectives should cover breadth of content, levels of learning, and affective outcomes. To an increasing extent, you will find it necessary to design objectives on an individual basis. If you are lucky, you will find that the objectives you devise are appropriate for most of the class. You will also find that some of the group have already mastered half or more of the knowledge, skills, and attitudes you expect them to take the entire term to learn. For these students you will need to devise useful activities and learning experiences. On the other hand, some of the group will not have the background needed to proceed with the learning planned for the majority. You must find some way of bringing these students up to the needed competence. In short, you have to devise individualized objectives for many, if not most, students. Even more unsettling is the realization that you will have to design a number of instructional strategies based on the objectives you have devised.

Instructional Strategies

In writing the instructional strategies to achieve your behavioral objectives, you have to find some way to take care of these students who are above and who are below the main body of the group. Usually this accommodation can best be accomplished by using such individualized materials as programmed units, cassettes with earphones, filmstrips with audio accompaniment, and other similar devices that can be used by a small group or by a single individual. Any of these devices requires previewing and planning on your part, and this means that your paper requires a great deal of research time to explore possible sources. But the time is well spent, for in the process you will broaden your own instructional repertoire. In describing the instructional strategies for the main body of your class, you should emphasize ways of modifying what you do as your successes and your failures come to light.

Evaluation of Success in Reaching Goals

Built into well-designed goals or objectives are ways of determining whether or not they have been achieved. In your lesson plans, whether for a term or a day, you will want to make the evaluation step clear and precise. The need for clarity in this area is particularly important when you are setting up individualized programs, but it is also necessary in working with the main group. Successful plans lead to successful lessons and successful learning. As you achieve your goals, you increase your own productivity and that of the profession. You also will have improved the learning of many students above the level they would have achieved if you had been less thorough in your preparation, instruction, and evaluation.

Part III

HOW TO WRITE A PAPER
IN EDUCATION

Content of the Paper

How to write a paper is divided into four sections: (1) content of the paper—what to say, (2) clarity in writing—how to say it, and (3) form of the paper—the mechanics of saying it and (4) documentation—how to give credit. This chapter will deal with content. In the section on organizing your material, the importance of a title was mentioned. The impact of the computer retrieval systems on sharpening the wording of the title was discussed. Titles that a computer can retrieve are usually good titles for readers too. Two examples that could be titles of small research studies described in the section on educational psychology will give you an idea about good and poor titles:

(good) Operant Conditioning to Control Swearing

(poor) A Study to Demonstrate How Operant Conditioning Can Be Used to Control Swearing

In the first title all of the words are key words that would be sorted by a computer. The reader also knows quickly what the study is all about. In the second title more than half of the words really do not improve the reader's understanding of the experiment. Here is another example from the same part of this text:

· (good) Classical Conditioning to Summon Mate

(poor) An Experiment to Test the Hypothesis That Classical Conditioning Can Be Used to Change the Behavior of a Mate at Meal Time

As you can see, all of the preceding remarks apply to these titles as well.

The paper you write is a report of the study you made, whether the study was based on the observation of children, an experimental manipulation of variables, or the analysis of studies made by others. Your report should be as clear and unambiguous as possible. It should describe exactly what was done, how it was done, and the conclusions that were reached as a result of making the study. The emphasis is on objectivity with as little bias as possible, so usually the report is written in the third person, referring to the author or the experimenter rather than to "I."

Before writing your report you should make an outline and jot down your points under different headings. Typically, your outline would cover the items listed below:

1. The topic (problem, purpose)
2. The finding (final hypothesis)
3. The background of the study—the library research, what others have said and done that bears on the topic
4. Your methods—what you actually did
5. Your findings (data)
6. Your conclusions and how were they derived
7. Your findings' use in teaching (optional)

Each of the points in the outline will be expanded in the following paragraphs.

THE TOPIC

The beginning provides the reader with a framework to understand all that follows. It defines the problem that has been studied and gives information about the purpose in studying this particular problem. You orient your reader in a few sentences so that his or her thinking can be adjusted to the kind of topic you will be describing. Often this section will describe a rather large field of study and the way in which you have carved out a small section that you have studied intensively.

THE FINDING

Right after you have defined what you did in the study you give the findings. You do not keep the reader in suspense about how the study turned out, but give the answer in the second section. This section of the report should be a clear statement that briefly tells whether you were successful or not in the task you set out to do. It bothers some students to give the answer in the beginning, especially if the answer is a qualified "maybe," but the reader can read the rest of the report critically to see what support you have for a conclusion already stated.

THE BACKGROUND OF THE STUDY

In this part of your report you detail what others have done in the same or related studies. This part of your paper needs documentation describing your sources exactly so that the reader can check to see how accurately you read other people's work. The next chapter describes many ways of documenting your sources. Papers are never complete in themselves; there are always studies that went before and that suggested ideas. All that we have written about reviewing the literature described the studying you need to do in order to write this section well.

YOUR METHODS

Methods are different for different kinds of papers, but in all of them you should describe exactly what you did so that other researchers could repeat your study just as you did it. The method section of your report is critically important. Often the reason a certain result comes out of one study and a different, sometimes opposite, result comes out of a similar study is that there were small differences in the methods followed in the two studies. You need to be specific in describing your sources of information, how the information was selected, and how the information was analyzed.

YOUR FINDINGS

These findings, or data, are the things you observed, or the results of the experiment you performed, or the findings that came out of your intensive library work. The findings are usually specific measurements, observations, or details that you have found. They should be as objective as you can make them.

YOUR CONCLUSIONS

Conclusions differ from findings—they are interpretations of the findings. They explain why the findings are significant. In your report you should explain why and how you decided that the conclusions were a logical outcome of your findings.

YOUR FINDINGS' USE IN TEACHING

Many research people claim that this section does not belong in a research report because it is likely to be subjective and colored by your prejudices. However, I think research studies should serve a practical purpose. You should see that what you have spent time doing should make a difference in what happens in the classroom. If you include a section in your report on utilizing the findings, you will think about how these results can make a difference and will be more likely to remember and use what you have learned.

Clarity in Writing

I have found over the years that there are some writing problems that keep cropping up either in my own work or in that of my students, and in this chapter I would like to review some of the more common points of usage and style. This review is by no means intended to be a complete course in English composition but simply a listing of most of the points that you may need to check as you are writing. You will already know most of them, but others may have become hazy over the years.

SAY IT CONCISELY AND EFFECTIVELY

Your papers in education are intended to inform the reader about your library or empirical research. In writing, your aim should be to say what you must say with clarity and precision. You must cover your topic thoroughly, but you must not go beyond it or repeat yourself needlessly. Sometimes students stop before they have covered all the points they should mention and leave it to the professor to fill in the blanks. Usually professors take a dim view of papers that require this kind of extrapolation on their part. The reading is harder, there is a note of uncertainty about whether the correct meaning has been interpreted, and furthermore, the professor probably feels a responsibility to insist on your expressing yourself properly. To summarize, you can be too cryptic in your presentation as well as too verbose. Your papers should explore your topic thoroughly without becoming redundant. But just as you should not stop writing too soon, neither should you go on too long. Say what needs to be said and then stop.

SHARPENING YOUR WRITING

Your words are joined into sentences and paragraphs. A few hints may make it possible for you to structure these basic elements of writing more effectively than you are accustomed to doing. One of my own problem points is illustrated in the preceding sentence. My first reaction was to stop the sentence after "effectively," but when you use the comparative "more" it must be followed by the term of the comparison, which is preceded by "than." Advertising copywriters are notoriously bad at violating this precept. They claim, "Car X gets more miles per gallon" and questions immediately arise: more than a camel? more than last year's model of the same make? or more than what? The point you want to make is clear to you, but it may not be clear to other people who may be reading your paper from a different frame of reference.

Paragraphs on One Topic

In high school you were taught that a paragraph should have one main idea that is elaborated. If you were not particularly interested when you were in school, this principle may have slipped past you as a formula without much meaning. Normally your paragraph should start with a topic sentence that tells what is going to be in the paragraph and that also links the paragraph to the one which precedes it. Many people who read a great deal as part of their work slip into reading the first sentence or two of a paragraph and then skipping to the last sentence, which is often used as a summary statement of what has gone before in the paragraph. If you realize that your professor may read what you have written quickly and not too carefully, you may find it desirable to use good lead-in sentences, to keep your paragraphs to a single topic, and to summarize what you have said so that it cannot be easily missed.

Variety in Sentence Structure

A simple sentence is one that consists of one subject and one predicate, either or both of which may be compound, such as, "The man hit the dog." A paper that consists only of sentences of this type makes pretty dull reading. The sentence about the man and the dog can be made more interesting and informative by adding adjectives describing the man or the dog or adverbs telling about the nature of the hitting. But in technical papers, you must choose adjectives and adverbs with care so that they do not distort your meaning. It is all too easy to add emotional coloring that is not justified by the facts you are presenting. Sometimes you can add variety to a simple sentence by using the interrogative form. Exclamations are rarely justified in technical writing.

The easiest way to add variety to your sentences is to use more than one kind. Mix short explosive or emphatic sentences with longer, more definitive ones. Use compound sentences, which are joined by conjunctions such as "and" or "but." Use complex sentences in which the main clause is modified by an adjectival or an adverbial clause that clarifies the meaning you are trying to express. To hold the reader's attention, vary sentence openers. You can start with a modifying phrase or clause that will add interest to the way you are telling your story.

Another way to add variety is to use parallel structures in your sentences. Often you can be quite eloquent by making the parallel structures into a series of related ideas. The beginning, the middle, or the end of the sentence can be a suitable place for parallel expressions. Often infinitives can be useful to clarify, to define, or to exemplify what you are saying. Modifying the meaning, restricting the sample size, and selecting the subjects for an experimental study are important steps in making the study viable. None of these techniques should be used just to be "cute." All of them can make your report more interesting to read and can also give you a sense of power as you practice using them. Your main purpose, however, is to learn to express yourself so that your papers reflect the work you have done in preparing them. In a way your writing is the sales package in which you enclose your product—the research you have done. It pays you to make the package attractive.

Using the Precise Word

In the English language many words mean almost the same thing. This duplication makes it possible for you to avoid using the same work repeatedly. The richness of the language also demands that you take care to see that the word you use is just the one you want to use. A good dictionary can be of a great help if you use it carefully. A copy of Roget's *Thesaurus of English Words and Phrases* can assist in finding exactly the right word to use and also in finding synonyms to replace words that are losing their freshness, but check a word that is new to you by looking it up in a dictionary. As you use adjectives and adverbs, remember that these words often carry emotional coloration in addition to their literal meaning. Would you prefer to be referred to as a *virile* man or a *big* man? a *vibrant* woman or a *healthy* woman? Think what happens when you make it a *healthy female*. You can change the meaning of what you are writing by a few changes in words that alter the emotional tone. Of course you can also brighten up your writing in the same way. The problem is to write so that people want to read your work and so that it both says and implies the correct meaning.

Avoiding Indefinite Referents

A number of words function as both pronouns and adjectives. Some of these words are particularly susceptible to uses that make the meaning of your writing quite unclear. This, that, these, and those are probably used more commonly as pronouns with indefinite referents than any others, although other pronouns sometimes are poorly used in referring to an obscure idea. I am often tempted to use the word *this* to refer to an idea in a previous sentence. *This* makes reading slower than it need be. In the previous sentence the pronoun *this* really refers to "the improper use of pronouns with indefinite referents" but an analysis to determine the referent of a pronoun to the preceding noun would indicate that it should refer to "sentence." It also might refer to "idea," to the infinitive "to use," or to the whole sentence. The preceding sentence would be clearer and easier to understand if it were rewritten to become, "The use of indefinite referents makes reading slower than it need be." You can sharpen your writing more quickly by eliminating the indefinite referents than by any other single change.

Form of the Paper

For your own satisfaction, for ease in reading, and for better grades, it is essential that you carefully prepare the paper before you submit it. Professors and graduate assistants are human; they make subjective evaluations of your paper, although they may not admit this fact even to themselves. Sharp format will not raise a "C" paper to an "A," but it will often make a "B+" into an "A−" and that difference is a third of a grade point, a difference that has meant admission or denial by a graduate school.

In all matters of form, listen to the directions given by your instructor. If he has rules that vary from what follows, by all means use his rules; but if you are left on your own, the following pattern should be of help. Start with a title page (Figure 9), on which you put the title in capital letters about three inches from the top of the page—if the title is more than one line long center it about three inches from the top. Put "by" and your name about six inches from the top of the page and center the course number, instructor, and date about three inches from the bottom of the paper. You center typing on a page by using the typewriter rule to locate the center of the line and backspacing half the number of letters and spaces in your title, name, heading, or whatever you want centered.

In any but very major papers, dedications, acknowledgements, and prefaces are usually omitted. A table of contents is useful in long papers, theses, and dissertations. The form of the table of contents found at the beginning of this book is satisfactory. A page listing figures and another listing tables is often

TITLE OF YOUR PAPER

by

Your Name

Education 212
Psychological Foundations of Education
Dr. J. A. R. Wilson
December 10, 1976

Figure 9 Sample Title Page

useful to the reader although, again, these pages would be found only in long papers.

TYPING THE BODY OF THE REPORT

The standard instructions for typing the body of the report are to leave margins of 1″ on the top, right, and bottom of the page and to leave a margin of 1½″ on the left. The extra space on the left makes it possible to bind the paper without making the text unreadable. Use 8½ × 11 inch white typing paper.

The paper should be double-spaced with a five-space indentation for paragraphs. Quotes longer than two lines may be indented three spaces and typed single-spaced and without quotation marks. Shorter quotes are included in the body of the text and are enclosed in quotation marks. Poetry is normally indented and single spaced since it is usually quoted material. Errors in typing should be corrected using coated correction paper such as KO-REC-TYPE or using a white paint corrector such as Liquid Paper Correction Fluid.

HEADINGS

Headings are used to make it easier for the reader to follow your presentation. Ordinarily, headings in the body of the text reflect the points in your outline and are set off in somewhat similar ways. Normally there will be at least two subheadings under any topic that is subdivided at all. Either the material is important enough to require another major heading or it is an extension of the principal topic of the heading.

Normally there is text material after each heading; that is, there should be at least one intervening paragraph between main heading and subheading. A rule of thumb is that paragraphs should have at least three sentences, although some reputable authors manage to make a single sentence so long that the reader is not surprised that it makes up a whole paragraph. Be warned that your professor is likely to mark you down for writing such sentences. It is safest to keep what you are saying straightforward, clear, and as understandable as you can make it.

In addition to the CHAPTER TITLE, ordinarily put into all capitals, three headings will usually cover all topics that are necessary. The most common arrangement is a center heading, a marginal heading, and a paragraph heading. Normally I use a center heading set off by three spaces above and below it. I capitalize initial letters but do not underline the heading (see example below).

Center Heading

After making the main points about the center heading, I often move on to a marginal heading. Under some circumstances no marginal headings are necessary and the next heading is another center heading. The decision depends upon the outline and just how the argument is being developed.

Marginal Heading

The marginal heading usually is underlined and written in capitals and lower case. There should be more than one marginal heading under a center heading.

Paragraph Headings: These can be set off in different ways, but I normally use this style. The heading is indented as a regular paragraph is indented, it is followed by a colon, and it is underlined. Some people prefer a period to a colon after the heading. You can vary these things to suit yourself as long as you are consistent. A person should be able to go through your paper, copy the center headings, put under each the marginal heading, and under each of those the paragraph headings and come up with your outline for the paper. The marginal headings should be subordinate to the center heading, and the paragraph headings should be subordinate to the marginal headings.

ILLUSTRATIONS AND FIGURES

Illustrations and figures are visual ways of explaining the ideas in the body of the text. They are not used just for decoration or to add independent interest to the paper. Illustrations can be cartoons or other similar figures, or they may be actual photographs either in black and white or in color. Figures normally are graphs. They may be of the bar, line, or pie type.

Using Illustrations

In some studies, sucn as growth and development, where observation is important, pictures can be an important way of sharpening your term paper. When only a single copy of the paper is being prepared, the picture can be mounted and captioned as part of the text. Polaroid cameras let you see what you have while you can still take another picture if you need one to make your point. The pictures can be mounted with rubber cement, which does not shrink or wrinkle the paper.

One difficulty in mounting actual photographs is that it makes the pages thick and bulky. This problem can be avoided by having the original copied on one of the new copiers such as the Xerox 6500, which will copy color, or the Xerox 3100, 4000, or 9200, which will copy black and white pictures. These copies will make it possible to include illustrations in papers where more than one copy is needed, and for much less time and money than has been necessary in the past. Many of these machines have only recently come on the market. In fact, it may take a phone call or two to the manufacturer's office to find someone who can do the duplicating for you.

Using Figures

Illustrations make a very large difference in certain kinds of papers, but nearly all reports can be made clearer by using one or more figures to illustrate the data that has been collected. Figures should be drawn carefully, using a pen with black ink. Squared paper that is printed in light blue can be photographed for reproduction without the squares showing. The figure should provide all the data necessary to interpret the drawing. Captions and legends should be clear. Lettering should be done either on the typewriter or with a lettering guide, unless you are particularly skilled in freehand lettering. Figures should be fitted into the text so that they illustrate the points under

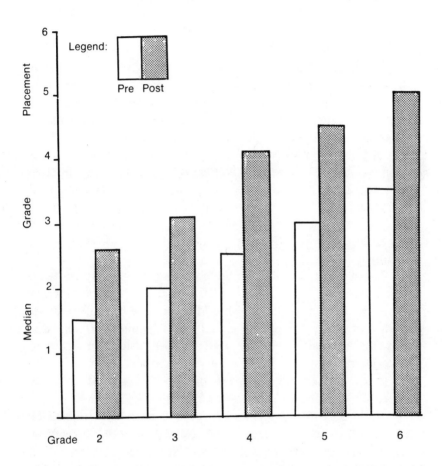

Figure 10 Bar Graph Showing Median Gains over Seven Months between Pretests and Posttests on the Wide Range Achievement Tests in Reading

discussion as smoothly as possible. Normally they are placed at the top of a page, the bottom of a page, or between paragraphs on a page. Figures 10 and 11 illustrate pre and post scores on the Wide Range Achievement Test for Reading. The subjects were Title I, E.S.E.A. pupils in a medium sized city.

TABLES

Figures are usually graphic representations of the data found in tables. Some people find it easier to interpret tables; others find figures more informative. In a report, tables should be presented close to the figures that represent them so that an interested reader can move from the table to the figure with as little difficulty as possible. Normally you will put your table on the paper so that it can be read as part of the text. In some cases the table may be too wide to fit within the six inches of text space. In that case, you may be able to get it all on the page by turning the page sideways. If so, the bottom of the table becomes the right margin when the pages are assembled.

The word *Table* and the table number are usually centered and on the next line is the title of the table, which is centered separately. Column headings should be concise but informative. Labels for rows, sometimes called stubs, should be clear and easily understood. Lines are used to make the data easier to read. There has been a tendency to reduce the number of lines used, since they increase the cost of reproducing the material.

Table 3, which contains the data from which Figures 10 and 11 were drawn, shows how the data can be presented. More lines are used in this illustration than you may find necessary, but the vertical lines help avoid difficulty with the column headings. Your headings may be simpler and may not need to be separated by lines. The horizontal lines are included in this example as a way of making it easier to follow the rows.

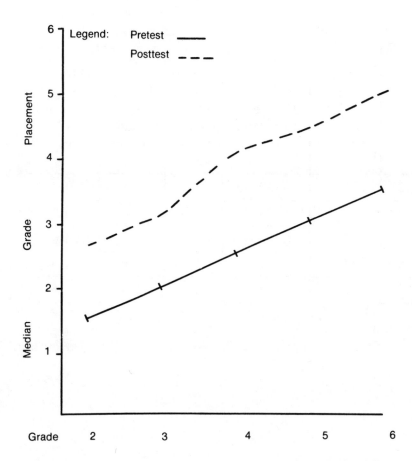

Figure 11 Line Graph Showing Median Gains over Seven Months between Pretests and Posttests on the Wide Range Achievement Tests in Reading

Table 3

Reading Gains
Wide Range Achievement Tests

Grade	Months Between Pre- & Post-test	No. of Students Who Rec'd Both Pre- & Posttests	Test Results Expressed as Median Grade Placements		
			Median Pre-test Grade Place-ment	Median Post-test Grade Place-ment	Difference Subtract Pre from Post Scores
2	7	62	1.5	2.6	1.1
3	7	73	2.1	3.1	1.0
4	7	55	2.5	4.1	1.6
5	7	67	3.0	4.5	1.5
6	7	48	3.5	5.0	1.5

Documentation

When you quote the work of someone else, you must give credit to the original author. Quite frequently you will want to lend strength to your argument by referring to another's work that relates to the topic you are trying to develop. How to refer to the other person's work is to some extent a matter of choice, although there are a number of conventions that offer guidelines. In my own work I use the American Psychological Association system. This prescribes the use of a date, or a name and a date, to refer to an item in the bibliography, which is placed as an appendix at the end of the book. You may have noticed these references in earlier parts of this book. Although the present volume is informal in tone and very like an essay in style, I use the same method of documentation in writing formal textbooks and research reports. Many authors prefer to use footnotes supported by bibliographic references, and many professors require you to write papers using footnotes. Kalvelage, Segal, and Anderson have done a fine job of pulling together the conventions with regard to documentation for this series of research guides, and the rest of this chapter reflects their *Research Guide for Undergraduates in Political Science* (1972).

FOOTNOTES

Few aspects of writing cause as much confusion, bewilderment, and frustration as the proper use of footnotes. Footnotes can be an essential part of scholarly writing, but until the fundamentals of their use are mastered, the footnote requirement can be a constant source of frustration. As a writing device footnotes are useful because they allow important information to be communicated without overburdening the text. More specifically, footnotes allow a writer to reflect both credit and blame where they are due by showing the source of facts and ideas, thereby permitting the reader to utilize cited sources. In addition, footnotes act as a helpful context for presenting information, indicating sources from which it came, and thus allowing the reader to judge the possible bias of such sources. Finally, footnotes allow a writer to discuss interesting sidelights of the material without breaking the flow of writing.

Two questions invariably arise whenever footnotes are required:

1. What should be footnoted?
2. What form is correct, particularly if unusual or specialized material is being used, such as mimeographed reports put out by a school district?

WHAT TO FOOTNOTE

While most style manuals or term-paper handbooks deal with footnote form, few ever touch upon the more difficult and confusing questions, such as "What kind of source should I footnote and how often should I do it?" There are no ready answers to this question and unfortunately it is quite easy to succumb to excess in either direction. If you feel uneasy about an assignment, the material, or the professor's standards and expectations, it is quite tempting to "over-document" a paper or to hang footnotes on it as though you were decorating a Christmas tree. This approach can be quite hazardous, for besides wasting time, the reader is overburdened with needless side trips to the bottom of the page and the likelihood of making technical errors is increased. Such errors would, of course, detract from the substance of a paper. Unnecessary footnotes, far from being a safeguard, can become a real problem.

Equally hazardous is the practice of "under-documentation." If footnoting has always been a mystery, something to be avoided, the possibility arises that the material will be distorted: important points may be omitted in order to avoid documentation, or the source of information and ideas may be left to the reader's imagination, implying that the work of others is somehow your own. Between these two unfortunate extremes three styles of scholarship are defined: the original scholar, the scholarly summarizer, and the essayist and journalist. The style which most closely approximates the assigned type of paper should be followed.

The *original scholar* form is appropriate for Ph.D. dissertations, Masters theses, honors papers, or term papers which fulfill the major portion of the requirements of a course. This style should also be used for papers consisting mainly of scholarly research from primary sources.

The *scholarly summarizer* style is appropriate for more frequently assigned term papers, which fulfill a minor portion of the requirements for a course. This type of paper usually consists of a summary, interpretation, and synthesis of secondary sources.

The *essayist and journalist* style is also appropriate for many types of term papers, but in such cases the emphasis is upon the writer's own experience or interpretation. Strictly speaking, there are few ideas which are completely new; however, if the emphasis is to be on an original and creative reaction of these ideas, and not the ideas themselves or their origin, the essayist style is appropriate. This style may also be used if the paper is primarily a personal account or a narrative of events witnessed or situations in which the writer participated.

Table 4 summarizes the use of footnotes for each of the styles of scholarship.

Quotations

There is little question concerning the footnoting of direct quotations. The *original scholar* and the *scholarly summarizer* almost always footnote direct quotations. The exception for

Table 4 / Three Types of Scholarship and Appropriate Footnote Use

Type of Information	Original Scholar	Scholarly Summarizer	Essayist and Journalist
Quotations	All except those quotations of common knowledge, in which case they would still be footnoted if they varied from one edition to another.	Same as original scholar.	Only if the quotation is controversial or highly significant to the text in which case the reference would be incorporated into the body of the material.
Facts 1. Controversial 2. Significant to the paper 3. Obscure	All but those which are part of common knowledge.	All controversial facts, a representative amount of significant facts to indicate the nature of sources, and only obscure facts which are central to the meaning of the paper.	Only controversial facts central to the meaning of the paper.
Commentary and Interpretation 1. Methodology	Brief bibliographical essay showing the scope of material.	Refers to other works which would contain bibliographical essays.	Only if different but similar methodology would yield significantly different results.
2. Context of opinions and sources	Brief bibliographical essay showing scope of material.	Refers to other works which would contain bibliographical essays.	Only to indicate that the author is aware of major different approaches; can be incorporated into the text.
Tangential information	Use infrequently for points which might need amplification. Generally, if it is worth writing, it should be included in the body of the text.	Only for points the absence of which might distort the meaning of the work. Again, it is preferable to place the information in the body of the text.	Rarely used except for humor.

even the most scholarly styles are quotations from such items of public domain as the Bible and the Constitution. In such cases it is permissible to incorporate a general reference into the text of the material.

EXAMPLE:

> There seemed little question that the proposal violated the "Separation of Church and State clause," the First Amendment to the Constitution.
> The father saw himself obeying the biblical admonition of "Spare the rod and spoil the child."

Form for quotations is covered in the next section.

The *essayist and journalist* make even greater use of the device of incorporating general references into the body of the text.

Facts

The *original scholar* footnotes all but the most obvious facts. If in doubt, ask if the average mature reader would automatically be aware of the origin and authenticity of a particular fact. If not, it should be footnoted. In general, the three criteria for footnoting facts are

1. *Controversiality*: Could honest men disagree over the authenticity or significance of this fact?
2. *Significance* to the paper: Does a significant part of your argument rest upon this fact?
3. *Obscurity*: Are the means or sources for establishing the authenticity of this fact beyond the average reader's experience or recall?

If a fact could be questioned in a scholarly paper on the basis of any of these three criteria, it should be footnoted. The *scholarly summarizer* needs to footnote only a representative sampling of his significant facts. In this way, the type of sources used is indicated. Obscure facts need not be footnoted unless they are central to the significance of the paper.

The *essayist and journalist* seldom footnote facts unless they are both controversial and significant to the basic purpose of the paper.

Commentary and Interpretation

Not every individual will read a report with the same interest. Some readers will be interested only in the main conclusions and the general thread of ideas whereas others will be interested in exploring in depth various aspects of the supporting evidence. Other readers will want to read the interesting sidelights found in research; some will find these sidelights a definite distraction. How is it possible for one manuscript to please such widely varying tastes?

Footnotes which comment upon and interpret data can be a partial solution to this dilemma. Such footnotes can be used for supplementary information, which will be of interest to some readers. Again, the use of such footnotes varies with the style of scholarship. The *original scholar* does not want to overburden the text with a full explanation of the development of his or her methodology. In order to understand the methodology fully it is also important to make the scope of articles in journals or books dealing with this metholology available to the reader. Such an explanation takes the form of the bibliographical footnote.

EXAMPLE:

Cf. Albert J. Harris, "Perceptual Difficulties in Reading Disability," in *Changing Concepts of Reading Instruction*, J. Allen Figurel (Ed.) (International Reading Conference Proceedings, VI, 1961), pp. 281-290; Katrina deHirsch, "Psychological Correlates in the Reading Process," in *Challenge and Experiment in Reading*, J. Allen Figurel (Ed.) (International Reading Association Conference Proceedings, VII, 1962), pp. 218-226; A. L. Drew, "A Neurological Appraisal of Familial Congenital Word-Blindness," *Brain*, *79* (1950), 440-460. (Harris 1968, p. 169.)

Tangential Information

The *original scholar* also can use footnotes to provide tangential information, as in the following:

EXAMPLE:

> When reading the *Hansard* report of a speech I had listened to in Parliament the day before, I used to find it impossible not to slow down to the pace of the speaker and to "hear" his very words. In the case of the late Sir Winston Churchill, notwithstanding the delay of many years and the fact that I might not have been present, I still slow down and seem to "hear" his voice. Further examples of this type of vestigial carry-over from the auditory element to the visual will be found in *Learning to Read*, an address I gave to the Royal Society of Arts, *Journal of the Royal Society of Arts, 109*, 149-180, London, 1961.

Methodology
Context of Opinions and Sources

Where the *original scholar* uses footnotes to present a short bibliographical essay on the sources, the *scholarly summarizer* uses footnotes to point to the location of such documentation in other sources. This identification of other sources is equally useful for both library and empirical research.

EXAMPLES:

> From Donald Light, Jr. and Robert S. Laufer, "College Youth: Psychohistory and Perspectives," in *Youth: The Seventy-fourth Yearbook of the National Society for the Study of Education* Part I, Robert J. Havighurst and Philip H. Dreyer (Eds.) (Chicago: University of Chicago Press, 1975), p. 103.

> From its earliest stages, the New Left was concerned about the quality of personal life and the importance of one's

inner world. This concern flourished and matured into the theme of "liberation" and the inner alternate forms of consciousness. See Richard Flacks, *Youth and Social Change* (Chicago: Markham, 1971); Charles Reich, *The Greening of America* (New York: Random House, 1970); and Michael Rossman, *The Wedding Within the War* (Garden City, New York: Doubleday, 1971).

From Bruce Joyce, "Conceptions of Man and Their Implications for Teacher Education," in *Teacher Education: The Seventy-fourth Yearbook of the National Society for the Study of Education* Part II, Kevin Ryan, (Ed.) (Chicago: University of Chicago Press, 1975), p. 128.

For an analysis of the extrapolation of cognitive psychology to curriculum, see Edmund V. Sullivan, *Piaget and the School* (Toronto: Ontario Institute for Studies in Education, 1967). For an advocacy position, and empirical investigations, see Irving Sigel and Frank Hooper, (Eds.), *Logical Thinking in Children* (New York: Holt, Rinehart and Winston, 1968).

FOOTNOTE AND BIBLIOGRAPHY FORM

Concerning footnote and bibliography forms one can justifiably be arbitrary. There is no inherent reason to use one form rather than another, except for the sake of clear communication and consistency. The works used should be cited in the same form as that used in indexes, bibliographies, or library card catalogs. In this way, a reader will be able to locate cited sources.

Following are examples of the types of footnotes and bibliographies most frequently used in education papers. I have included the kind of text reference used when footnotes are not used as well as a number of comments and explanations that should be helpful to you. Most of the forms are based on the *Publication Manual of the American Psychological Association*, 2nd. ed., which is the form most commonly followed in research papers and textbooks in education. This manual capitalizes only the initial word and the word following a colon in the titles in the bibliography.

I would like to emphasize that the process of referencing your statements is important but that the exact form varies slightly from place to place. The purpose of referencing is to make it possible for someone else to find your reference and check it for accuracy of both content and significance. One variable that is still in flux is the way of recording the name of the author. The *Publication Manual of the American Psychological Association* states that the correct form is to use initials only. The other volumes in this series say "author's full name." A tradition had grown up of using initials with men and first names with women authors. I am sure you can see why this practice drew fire from women authors and teachers. I favor using names as they are given on the title page of the book, article, or other material. Some authors are well-known by their initials, for instance, B. F. Skinner, the psychologist; others are known by their given names, for instance, Albert J. Harris, the reading specialist. While mixing the style of recording names is not neat and tidy, it does make the search for sources more meaningful and therefore better than any single rule. Your bibliography should contain only materials that were referred to in the text. Some students like to impress the professor by including materials in the bibliography that have not been used. This practice is generally frowned on by professors.

Footnotes, General Rules

Books should include

1. Author's full name
2. Complete title
3. Editor, compiler, or translator (if any)
4. Name of series, volume or series number (if any)
5. Number of volumes
6. City, publisher, and date
7. Volume number and page number

Articles should include

1. Author
2. Title of article
3. Periodical
4. Volume of periodical
5. Date and page numbers of article

Unpublished material should include
1. Author
2. Title (if any)
3. Type of material
4. Location
5. Date
6. Page number (if any)

Bibliography, General Rules

Footnote style can be changed to bibliographic style by transposing author's first and last names, removing parentheses from facts of publication, omitting page references, and repunctuating with periods instead of commas.

Books should include

1. Name of author(s) or institutions responsible
2. Full title, including subtitle if one exists; edition if not the original
3. Editor, compiler, or translator (if any)
4. Volume number
5. Name of series
6. Publisher's name, city (state)
7. Date of publication

Articles should include

1. Name of author
2. Title of article
3. Name of periodical
4. Volume number (or date, or both)
5. Page numbers of article

Unpublished material should include

1. Author
2. Title (if any)
3. Type of material
4. Location
5. Date
6. Page number (if any)

Examples Contrasting Footnote and Bibliographic Forms

Book with One Author
FOOTNOTE: 1. Jeanne S. Chall, *Learning to Read: The Great Debate* (New York: McGraw-Hill, 1967), p. 89.

BIBLIOGRAPHY: Chall, Jeanne S. *Learning to read: The great debate.* New York: McGraw-Hill, 1967.

Book with Two Authors
FOOTNOTE: 2. Mildred C. Robeck and John A. R. Wilson, *Psychology of Reading: Foundations of Instruction* (New York: John Wiley & Sons, 1974), p. 180.

BIBLIOGRAPHY: Robeck, Mildred C., and Wilson, John A. R. *Psychology of reading: Foundations of instruction.* New York: John Wiley & Sons, 1974.

Book with Three Authors
FOOTNOTE: 3. John A. R. Wilson, Mildred C. Robeck, and William B. Michael, *Psychological Foundations of Learning and Teaching*, 2nd. ed. (New York: McGraw-Hill, 1974), p. 465.

BIBLIOGRAPHY: Wilson, John A. R., Robeck, Mildred C., & Michael, William B. *Psychological foundations of learning and teaching* (2nd. ed.). New York: McGraw-Hill, 1974.
Comment: Text insert: (1974) or (Wilson, Robeck, and Michael, 1974).

Book with More Than Three Authors
FOOTNOTE: 4. B. S. Bloom et al., *Taxonomy of Educational Objectives: The Cognitive Domain: Handbook I* (New York: Longmans, Green, 1956), p. 76.

BIBLIOGRAPHY: Bloom, B. S., Engelhart, M. D., Furst, E. J., Hill, W. H., & Krathwohl, D. R. *Taxonomy of educational objectives: The cognitive domain. Handbook I.* New York: Longmans, Green, 1956.
Comment: Note that the footnote uses "et al." but the bibliography gives all authors.

Book with an Association as Author
FOOTNOTE: 5. Educational Testing Service, *Let's Look at First Graders: A Guide to Understanding and Fostering Intellectual Development in Young Children* (New York: Board of Education, 1965), p. 5.
BIBLIOGRAPHY: Educational Testing Service. *Let's look at first graders: A guide to understanding and fostering intellectual development in young children.* New York: Board of Education, 1965.
Comment: Text insert: (1965) or (Educational Testing Service, 1965).

Book with Corporate Author
FOOTNOTE: 6. U. S. Government Printing Office, *Style Manual*, rev. ed. (Washington, D.C.: Author, 1973), p. 7.
BIBLIOGRAPHY: U.S. Government Printing Office. *Style manual* (Rev. ed.). Washington, D.C.: Author, 1973.
Comment: Alphabetize under U.S. government.

Author's Name Not on Title Page but Known
FOOTNOTE: 7. [Harold Benjamin,] *The Sabre-tooth Curriculum* (New York: McGraw-Hill, 1939), p. 78.
BIBLIOGRAPHY: [Benjamin, Harold.] *The sabre-tooth curriculum.* New York: McGraw-Hill, 1939.

Book, No Author
FOOTNOTE: 8. *Mathematics in Type* (Richmond, Va.: Byrd Press, 1954), p. 2.
BIBLIOGRAPHY: *Mathematics in type.* Richmond, Va: Byrd Press, 1954.
Comment: Text insert: (*Mathematics in Type*, 1954).

Books in Translation

FOOTNOTE: 9. Jean Piaget, *La Formation du Symbole Chez l'Enfant* (Neuchâtel: Delachaux et Niestlé, 1946. C. Gattegno and F. M. Hodgson [translators] *Play Dreams and Imitation in Childhood*, New York: Norton, 1951), p. 16.

BIBLIOGRAPHY: Piaget, Jean. *La formation du symbole chez l'enfant*. Neuchâtel: Delachaux et Niestlé, 1946. (Trans. by) C. Gattegno and F.M. Hodgson. *Play, dreams, and imitation in childhood*. New York: Norton, 1951.

Comment: Text insert: (Piaget 1946/1951). Note: Many bibliographies show Piaget and the English title and publication without translator.

Edited Volumes

FOOTNOTE: 10. N. L. Gage (Ed.), *Hankbook of Research on Teaching* (Chicago: Rand McNally, 1963), p. vi.

BIBLIOGRAPHY: Gage, N. L. (Ed.). *Handbook of research on teaching*. Chicago: Rand McNally, 1963.

Author within an Edited Volume

FOOTNOTE: 11. John C. Snidecor, Helping the Child Who Stutters, in John A. R. Wilson (Ed.), *Diagnosis of Learning Difficulties* (New York: McGraw-Hill, 1971), p. 88.

BIBLIOGRAPHY: Snidecor, John C. Helping the child who stutters, in John A. R. Wilson (Ed.) *Diagnosis of learning difficulties*. New York: McGraw-Hill, 1971. pp. 83-95.

Comment: Text insert: (Snidecor, 1971, p. 88). Note: The name of the editor(s) is not inverted in the bibliography.

New Edition, New Editor, Well-known Work

FOOTNOTE: 12. Paul H. Mussen (Ed.), *Carmichael's Manual of Child Psychology*, 3rd. ed. (New York: John Wiley & Sons, 1970), p. viii.

BIBLIOGRAPHY: Mussen, Paul H. (Ed.). *Carmichael's manual of child psychology* (3rd. ed.). New York: John Wiley & Sons, 1970.

Comment: Text insert: (Mussen, 1970, p. viii). Note: Editor's name is inverted to fit indexing.

Volume in a Series
 FOOTNOTE: 13. E. Aronson, Some Antecedents of
Interpersonal Attraction (in W. J. Arnold and D. Levine [Eds.],
Nebraska Symposium on Motivation [Vol. 17], Lincoln:
University of Nebraska Press, 1969), p. 48.
 BIBLIOGRAPHY: Aronson, E. Some antecedents of in-
terpersonal attraction. In W. J. Arnold & D. Levine (eds.).
Nebraska symposium on motivation (Vol. 17). Lincoln: Uni-
versity of Nebraska Press, 1969.
 Comment: Text insert: (Aronson, 1969, p. 48).

Citation from a Secondary Source
 FOOTNOTE: 14. Metropolitan Life Insurance, How Old
Are You? (In P. H. Mussen and J. J. Conger, *Child Development
and Personality* [New York: Harper & Row, 1956], p. 317).
 BIBLIOGRAPHY: Mussen, Paul H., & Conger, J. J. *Child
development and personality*. New York: Harper & Row, 1956.
 Comment: Text insert: (Metropolitan Life Insurance, How Old
Are You? cited in Mussen and Conger, 1956, p. 317). Note:
This reference is more available in Mussen and Conger than in
any other source.

Paperback Edition of a Book
 FOOTNOTE: 15. Aaron Wildavsky, *The Politics of the
Budgetary Process* (Boston: Little, Brown, paperback, 1964). p.
177.
 BIBLIOGRAPHY: Wildavsky, Aaron. *The politics of the
budgetary process*. Boston: Little, Brown, paperback, 1964.

Introduction to Book by Another Author
 FOOTNOTE: 16. Jean Piaget, Introduction to *Piaget and
Knowledge*, by Hans G. Furth (Englewood Cliffs, N.J.: Prentice-
Hall, 1969), p. vi.
 BIBLIOGRAPHY: Piaget, Jean. Introduction to *Piaget
and knowledge*, by Hans G. Furth. Englewood Cliffs, N.J.:
Prentice-Hall, 1969.
 Comment: Text insert: (Piaget, 1969, p. vi).

Book Review

FOOTNOTE: 17. Roger F. Aubrey, review of *P.S. 2001: The Story of the Pasadena Alternative School* by Philip H. DeTurk, *The Personnel and Guidance Journal*, 1975, *53*, 803-804.

BIBLIOGRAPHY: Aubrey, Roger F. Review of *P.S. 2001: The story of the pasadena alternative school* by Philip H. DeTurk. *The Personnel and Guidance Journal*, 1975, *53*, 803-804.

Journal Article with One Author

FOOTNOTE: 18. Duane M. Giannangelo, Make Report Cards Meaningful, *The Educational Forum*, 1975, *39*, 409-413.

BIBLIOGRAPHY: Giannangelo, Duane M. Make report cards meaningful. *The Educational Forum*, 1975, *39*, 409-413. Comment: Text insert: (Giannangelo, 1975). Note: When a journal is numbered for the complete volume there is no need for the number of the issue, but when each issue starts on page 1 the volume number is followed by the issue number in parentheses.

Journal Article with More than One Author

FOOTNOTE: 19. Annie W. Ward, Bruce W. Hall, and Charles F. Schramm, Evaluation of Published Educational Research: A National Survey, *American Educational Research Journal*, 1975, *12*, 109-128.

BIBLIOGRAPHY: Ward, Annie W., Hall, Bruce W., & Schramm, Charles F. Evaluation of published educational research: A national survey. *American Educational Research Journal*, 1975, *12*, 109-128. Comment: Text insert: (Ward, Hall, and Schramm, 1975).

Journal Article with Corporate Author

FOOTNOTE: 20. Le Dix-huitième Congrès de l'AIPA, *International Review of Applied Psychology*, 1975, *24*, 7-8.

BIBLIOGRAPHY: Le dix-huitième congrès de l'AIPA. *International Review of Applied Psychology*, 1975, *24*, 7-8. Comment: Text insert: (1975). Alphabetize under Dix.

Magazine Article with Discontinuous Pages

FOOTNOTE: 21. Joseph Adelson, Battered Pillars of the American System: Education, *Fortune*, April 1975, pp. 140-141, 143, 145.

BIBLIOGRAPHY: Adelson, Joseph. Battered pillars of the american system: Education. *Fortune*, April 1975, pp. 140-141, 143, 145.

Comment: Text insert: (Adelson, 1975). Note: Magazines are identified by issue date rather than volume number.

Magazine Article with No Author

FOOTNOTE: 22. Budge Cuts: The New Campus Issue, *Time*, May 12, 1975, p. 48.

BIBLIOGRAPHY: Budget cuts: The new campus issue. *Time*, May 12, 1975, p. 48.

Comment: Text insert: (Budget Cuts, 1975). Note: When the volume is not used "p." or "pp." is inserted before the numbers of the pages. "Vol." and "pp." are not used when the volume number is italicized.

Newspaper Article with No Author, Discontinuous Pages

FOOTNOTE: 23. Sex Education Plan Reviewed, *Santa Barbara News-Press*, July 28, 1975, pp. B1, B2.

BIBLIOGRAPHY: Sex education plan reviewed. *Santa Barbara News-Press*, July 28, 1975, pp. B1, B2.

Comment: Text insert: (Sex Education, 1975).

Monograph with Issue Number and Serial Number

FOOTNOTE: 24. E. E. Maccoby and K. W. Konrad, The Effect of Preparatory Set on Selective Listening: Developmental Trends, *Monographs of the Society for Research in Child Development*, 1967, *32* (4, Serial No. 112).

BIBLIOGRAPHY: Maccoby, E. E., & Konrad, K. W. The effect of preparatory set on selective listening: Developmental trends. *Monographs of the Society for Research in Child Development*, 1967, *32*(4, Serial No. 112).

Comment: Text insert: (Maccoby and Konrad, 1967).

Monograph Published Separately

FOOTNOTE: 25. K. L. Smoke, An Objective Study of Concept Formation, *Psychological Monographs*, 1932, No. 191, p. 10.

BIBLIOGRAPHY: Smoke, K. L. An objective study of concept formation. *Psychological Monographs*, 1932, No. 191, p. 10.

Comment: Text insert: (Smoke, 1932). Note: Until 1966 *Psychological Monographs* were published as separate volumes; from 1967-1970 they were published as journal supplements; since 1971 they have been bound into the journals with continuous pagination.

Monograph Bound Separately as Supplement to a Journal

FOOTNOTE: 26. A. Paivio et al., Concreteness, Imagery, and Meaningfulness Values for 925 Nouns, *Journal of Experimental Psychology Monograph*, 1969, 76(1, pt.2).

BIBLIOGRAPHY: Paivio, A., Yuille, J. C., & Madigan, S. A. Concreteness, imagery, and meaningfulness values for 925 nouns. *Journal of Experimental Psychology Monograph*, 1968, 76(1, Pt. 2).

Monograph Bound into Journal with Continuous Pagination

FOOTNOTE: 27. A. R. Wagner et al., Rehearsal in Animal Conditioning, *Journal of Experimental Psychology*, 1973, *97*, 407-426 (Monograph).

BIBLIOGRAPHY: Wagner, A. R., Rudy, J. W., & Whitlow, J. W. Rehearsal in animal conditioning. *Journal of Experimental Psychology*, 1973, *97*, 407-426. (Monograph)

Abstract Used without Supporting Article

FOOTNOTE: 28. Benjamin R. Brandt, The New World of Business Communications, *Balance Sheet*, 1973, *55*, 148-149. (Abstract CIJE, EJ 089 171).

BIBLIOGRAPHY: Brandt, Benjamin R. The new world of business communications. *Balance Sheet*, 1973, *55*, 148-149. (Abstract CIJE, EJ 089 171)

Comment: This listing makes it possible to check the source used.

Doctoral Dissertations in *Dissertation Abstracts International*
    FOOTNOTE: 29. Harold I. Bock, Social Change and the Democratic Ideal (Doctoral dissertation, University of Oregon, 1973), *Dissertation Abstracts International*, 1974, *34*, 5572A.
    BIBLIOGRAPHY: Bock, Harold I. Social change and the democratic ideal (Doctoral dissertation, University of Oregon, 1973). *Dissertation Abstracts International*, 1974, *34*, 5572A. Comment: Text insert: (Bock, 1973). Note: *Dissertation Abstracts International* is a continuation of *Dissertation Abstracts.*

Unpublished Doctoral Dissertation Available from Library
    FOOTNOTE: 30. Dennis C. Russo, *Human vs Automated Instruction of Autistic Children.* Unpublished doctoral dissertation, University of California, Santa Barbara, 1975. p. 10.
    BIBLIOGRAPHY: Russo, Dennis C. *Human vs automated instruction of autistic children.* Unpublished doctoral dissertation, University of California, Santa Barbara, 1975.
Comment: Text insert: (Russo, 1975).

Reference Available from ERIC
    FOOTNOTE: 31. Harry Singer, *IQ Is not Related to Reading*, Denver, Colorado: paper read at International Reading Association, May 6, 1973. (ERIC Document Reproduction Service No. ED 088 004).
    BIBLIOGRAPHY: Singer, Harry. *IQ is not related to reading.* Denver, Colorado. Paper read at International Reading Association, May 6, 1973. (ERIC Document Reproduction Service No. ED 088 004).
Comment: Text insert: (Singer, 1973). Note: This is the kind of document that was very difficult to locate or use before the advent of ERIC.

Technical Report Available from the
National Technical Information Service (NTIS)
    FOOTNOTE: 32. M. A. Gordon and R. A. Bottenberg, *Prediction of Unfavorable Discharge by Separate Education Levels* (PRL-TRD-62-5), Lackland Airforce Base, Tex.: 6570th Per-

sonnel Research Laboratory, Aerospace Medical Division, April 1962. (NTIS No. AD-284 802)

BIBLIOGRAPHY: Gordon, M. A., & Bottenberg, R.A. *Prediction of unfavorable discharge by separate educational levels* (PRL-TRD-62-5). Lackland Air Force Base, Tex.: 6570th Personnel Research Laboratory, Aerospace Medical Division, April 1962. (NTIS No. AD-284 802)

Comment: Text insert: (Gordon and Bottenberg, 1962). Note: A great many research documents are available through various government archives.

Publications Available from the Government Printing Office

FOOTNOTE: 33. S. D. Clements, *Minimal Brain Dysfunction in Children* (NINDS Monograph No. 3, U.S. Public Health Service Publication No. 1415), Washington, D.C.: U.S. Government Printing Office, 1966.

BIBLIOGRAPHY: Clements, S. D. *Minimal brain dysfunction in children* (NINDS Monograph No. 3, U.S. Public Health Service Publication No. 1415), Washington, D.C.: U.S. Government Printing Office, 1966.

Mimeographed or Other Nonprinted Reports

FOOTNOTE: 34. John A. R. Wilson, Annual Evaluation Report: Basic Skills Development Project: Title I – E.S.E.A. mimeographed (Santa Barbara School District, Santa Barbara High School District, 1970), p. 86.

BIBLIOGRAPHY: Wilson, John A. R. Annual evaluation report: Basic skills development project: Title I – E.S.E.A. Mimeographed. Santa Barbara School District, Santa Barbara High School District, 1970.

Minutes of a Meeting: Not Reproduced

FOOTNOTE: 35. Minutes of Meeting Santa Barbara School District Board of Education, Santa Barbara, California, July 10, 1975, p. 2.

BIBLIOGRAPHY: Board of Education. Santa Barbara, California. Minutes of Meeting of July 10, 1975.

Comment: Text insert: (Board of Education, 1975). Note: Board of Education meetings are very useful in some research projects.

Paper Read or Speech Delivered at a Meeting

FOOTNOTE: 36. John A. R. Wilson, How Motivation Is Learned: A Neurological Explanation. (Paper given at Preconvention Institute 7: Brain Function in Reading and Reading Disability, International Reading Association, New York, May 12, 1975), p. 5.

BIBLIOGRAPHY: Wilson, John A. R. How motivation is learned: A neurological explanation. Paper given at Preconvention Institute 7: Brain Function in Reading and Reading Disability, International Reading Association, May 12, 1975, at New York City. Mimeographed.

Comment: Text insert: (Wilson, 1975).

Interview

FOOTNOTE: 37. Interview with Dr. Norman B. Sharer, Superintendent of Schools, Santa Barbara, California, May 8, 1972.

BIBLIOGRAPHY: Sharer, Norman B. Superintendent of Schools, Santa Barbara, California. Interview, May 8, 1972.

Comment: Text insert: (Sharer, 1972).

Letters

FOOTNOTE: 38. Mildred C. Robeck, letter dated July 7, 1975.

BIBLIOGRAPHY: Robeck, Mildred C. Personal communication. Dated July 7, 1975.

Radio and Television Programs

FOOTNOTE: 39. CBS, CBS News Special, August 3, 1975. A Tale of Two Irelands, Howard Stringer and John Lawrence, reporters.

BIBLIOGRAPHY: CBS, CBS News Special, August 3, 1975. A tale of two Irelands. Howard Stringer and John Lawrence, reporters.

Film

FOOTNOTES· 40. Ray Hosford (Producer), *Observing and Recording Behavior* (Washington, D.C.: American Personnel and Guidance Association Film Department, 1974, film).

BIBLIOGRAPHY: Hosford, Ray (Producer). *Observing and recording behavior.* Washington, D.C.: American Personnel and Guidance Association Film Department, 1974. (Film) Comment: Text insert: (Hosford, 1974).

These guidelines will provide you with a basis for handling most referencing you might have to do. If you want to use a document of a kind not listed above, the general principle is to reference it so that a person looking at your bibliography will be able to locate the reference with the least possible trouble. Text inserts have been shown for many of the reference styles above. If you use this method of documentation rather than footnotes, there are only two things to remember: (1) if the name is already in the sentence as in "Hosford (1974) produced a set of eight films to accompany *Behavioral Approaches to Counseling*," you need only the date in the insert; (2) if the name does not appear, as in, "A series of eight films was produced to accompany *Behavioral Approaches to Counseling*," (Hosford, 1974) use both the name and the date in the insert. Remember that your paper is intended to show what you know. Guides are only that and are intended as a help to make your paper writing easier and clearer.

Bibliography

Bayley, Nancy. The development of mental abilities. In Paul H. Mussen (Ed.) *Carmichael's manual of child psychology*. New York: John Wiley & Sons, 1970. Pp. 1163-1209.

Bloom, B.S., Engelhart, M. D., Furst, E. J., Hill, W. H., & Krathwohl, D. R. *Taxonomy of educational objectives: The cognitive domain. Handbook I*. New York: Longmans, Green, 1956.

Boehm, Eric H. (Ed.) *America: History and life: A guide to periodical literature*. Santa Barbara, California: Clio Press for the American Bibliographic Center, 1964- .

Boehm, Eric H. (Ed.) *Historical abstracts, 1775-1945: Bibliography of the world's periodical literature*. Santa Barbara, California: Clio Press with the International Social Science Institute, 1955- .

Buros, O. K. (Ed.) *The seventh mental measurements yearbook*. Highland Park, New Jersey: Gryphon Press, 1972. 2 Vols.

Chall, Leo P. (Ed.) *Sociological abstracts*. New York: Sociological Abstracts Inc., 1953- .

Coleman, J. S., Campbell, E. Q., Hobson, C. J., McPartland, J., Mood, A. M., Wienfield, F. D., & York, R. L. *Equality of educational opportunity*. Washington, D.C.: U. S. Government Printing Office, 1966.

Current index to journals in education: Mock-Up ERIC. Washington, D.C.: U. S. Government Printing Office, 1974.

Ehrenreich, Julia W., & Hewitt, Marylouise (Eds.) *Education index*. New York: H. W. Wilson, 1929- .

Fantz, R. L. Visual experience in infants: Decreased attention to familiar patterns relative to novel ones. *Science*, 1964, *146*, 668-670.

Flanders, H. A. Using interaction analysis in in-service training of teachers. *Journal of Experimental Education*, 1962, *30*, 313-316.

Gesell, A., Halverson, H. M., Thompson, H., Ilg, F. L., Castern, B. M., & Amatruda, C. S. *The first five years of life: A guide to the study of the preschool child*. New York: Harper & Row, 1940.

Gesell, A., & Ilg, F. L. (In collaboration with L. B. Ames & G. E. Bullis). *The child from five to ten*. New York: Harper & Row, 1946.

Gesell, A., Ilg, F. L., & Ames, L. B. *Youth: The years from ten to sixteen*. New York: Harper & Row, 1956.

Harris, Albert J. Diagnosis and remedial instruction in reading. In Helen M. Robinson (Ed.) *Innovation and change in reading instruction: The sixty-seventh yearbook of the National Society for the Study of Education*. Chicago: Distributed by the University of Chicago Press, 1968.

Joyce, Bruce. Conceptions of man and their implications for teacher education. In Kevin Ryan (Ed.) *Teacher education: The seventy-fourth yearbook of the National Society for the Study of Education*. Chicago: University of Chicago Press, 1975.

Kalvelage, C., Segal, M., & Anderson, P. J. *Research guide for undergraduates in political science*. Morristown, New Jersey: General Learning Press, 1972.

Light, Donald, Jr., & Laufer, Robert S. College youth: Psycho-history and perspectives. In Robert J. Havighurst & Philip H. Dreyer (Eds.) *Youth: The seventy-fourth yearbook of the National Society for the Study of Education*. Chicago: University of Chicago Press, 1975.

Palmermo, David S. (Ed.) *Child development abstracts and bibliography*. Chicago: University of Chicago Press, 1924- .

Piaget, Jean. *The construction of reality in the child*. New York: Basic Books, 1954.

Quintillian. Institutes of oratory (70 A.D.). In R. Ulick (Ed.) *Three thousand years of educational wisdom*. Cambridge, Mass.: Harvard University Press, 1954.

Research in education ERIC. Washington, D.C.: U. S. Government Printing Office, 1966- .

Research in education–Level 2 Mock-Up ERIC. Washington, D.C.: U. S. Government Printing Office, 1974.

Rosenthal, R., & Jacobson, Lenore. *Pygmalion in the classroom*. New York: Holt, Rinehart and Winston, 1968.

Swift, D. F. (Ed.) *Sociology of education abstracts*. Liverpool, England: Information for Education Ltd., 1964- .

Thesaurus of ERIC descriptors. New York: CCM Information Corporation, 1974.

Thorndike, E. L. *The psychology of learning (educational psychology II)*. New York: Teachers College Press, 1913.

Thorndike, Robert L. Review of *Pygmalion in the classroom* by R. Rosenthal and L. Jacobson. *American Educational Research Journal*, 1968, *5*, 708-711.

Torrance, E. P., & Arsan, K. Experimental studies of homogeneous and heterogeneous groups for creative scientific tasks. In W. W. Charters, Jr., & N. L. Gage (Eds.) *Readings in the social psychology of education*. Boston: Allyn & Bacon, 1963, pp. 133-140.

Trowbridge, M. H., & Cason, H. An experimental study of Thorndike's theory of learning. *Journal of Genetic Psychology*. 1932, 7, pp. 245-258.

White, Burton L. *Human infants: Experience and psychological development*. Englewood Cliffs, New Jersey: Prentice-Hall, 1971.

Wilson, John A. R., Robeck, Mildred C., & Michael, William B. *Psychological foundations of learning and teaching* (2nd ed.). New York: McGraw-Hill, 1974.

Wilson, John R. M. *Research guide in history*. Morristown, New Jersey: General Learning Press, 1974.

Wright, Thomas M. (Ed.) *Current index to journals in education ERIC*. New York: Macmillan Information, 1969- .

Index

Abstracts. *See also* Indexes
  America: History and Life, 62
  *Child Development Abstracts and
    Bibliography*, 52-53
  Dissertation Abstracts International,
    122
  Historical Abstracts, 1775-1945, 62
  Psychological Abstracts, 48-52
  Sociological Abstracts, 53-54
  Sociology of Education Abstracts, 54
Accession Number Cross Reference
    (RIE), 34-36
Affects, use of, 75
*America: History and Life: A Guide to
    Periodical Literature*, 62
American Psychological Association
  documentation system of, 105
  Psychological Abstracts published
    by, 48
  Publication Manual of, 112-113
Arsan, K., 66
Articles, footnote and bibliographic
    forms for, 119-120
Attitude scales, 68
Author Index (RIE), 34

Baselines
  in curriculum, 82
  in experimentation, 73
Bayley, Nancy, 7, 69
Behavioral objectives
  in curriculum, 83
  writing of, 76
Berkeley Growth Studies, 69

Biases, in literature, 19
Bibliographies. *See also* Abstracts;
    Indexes
  *Child Development Abstracts and
    Bibliography*, 52-53
  form for, 112-125
  general rules for, 114-115
  Historical Abstracts, 1775-1945, 62
  in literature searches, 16-17
  preparation of, 58
Bloom, B. S., 77-78
Book reviews, footnote and biblio-
    graphic forms for, 119
Books, footnote and bibliographic forms
    for, 115-118
Bronfenbrenner, Uri, 4
Buros, O. K., 55, 79

Cason, H., 72-73
*Child Development Abstracts and Bibli-
    ography*, 52-53
Child from Five to Ten, The (Gesell), 71
CIJE. *See Current Index to Journals in
    Education*
Classical conditioning experiments, 74-
    75
Classification systems, 23
  Dewey, 24-25
  Library of Congress, 25-27
Coleman, J. S., 65-66
Computer searches, 28
Conditioning in experimentation, 73-75
Counseling and guidance, papers in, 80-
    81

Cross-sectional studies, 69-70
Current Index to Journals in Education
(CIJE), 28, 36
counseling and guidance in, 81
Curriculum and methods, 9-11
papers in, 81-84
behavioral objectives in, 83
establishing baselines for, 82
instructional strategies in, 83-84

Development. *See* Growth and development
Dewey, Melvil, 24
Dewey decimal classification, 23, 24-25
Dissertation Abstracts International,
122
Doctoral dissertations, footnote and
bibliographic forms for, 122
Document Résumés (RIE), 29
Documentation in papers, 105-125
footnotes, 105-112
commentary and interpretation
in, 110
determination of, 106-107, 108
and facts, 109-110
and methodology, 111-112
and quotations, 107, 109
tangential information in, 111
footnote and bibliography form,
112-125

Economics of education, 6-7
papers in, 68-69
Education
in Dewey decimal classification,
24-25
economics of, 6-7, 68-69
history of, 5, 61-64
in Library of Congress classification,
26-27
philosophy of, 3-5, 60-61
psychology in, 8-9, 72-77
sociology of, 6, 64-67
Education Index, 36, 46-48
Educational psychology, 8-9
papers in, 72-77
Educational Resources Information
Center (ERIC) 28-46
footnote and bibliographic
forms for, 122
Educational sociology, papers in,
64-68
Effect, Law of, 72-73
Elements (Euclid), 62

ERIC. *See* Educational Resources Information Center
Euclid, 62
Evaluation. *See also* Measurement; Tests
and testing
measurement and, 77-79
of success in reaching goals, 84
Exercise, Thorndike's Law of, 72-73
Experimentation, 8-9
affects used in, 75
classical conditioning in, 74-75
operant conditioning in, 73-74

Facts, documentation of, 109-110
Fantz, R. L., 70
Figures in papers, 99-102
Films, footnote and bibliographic forms
for, 125
First Five Years of Life, The (Gesell), 71
Flanders, H. A., 67
Footnotes, 105-112
form for, 112-125
general rules for, 113-114

Gesell, Arnold, 7, 69-70, 71
Government Printing Office, footnote
and bibliographic forms for,
123
Group dynamics, 67
Growth and development, 7
Gesell on, 71
papers in, 69-71
Piaget on, 4, 70-71
Guidance. *See* Counseling and guidance

Headings in papers, 98-99
*Historical Abstracts, 1775-1945: Bibli-
ography of the World's Periodical Literature*, 62
History of education, 5
papers in, 61-64

Illustrations in papers, 99-102
Indexes
America: History and Life, 62
*Child Development Abstracts and
Bibliography*, 52-53
CIJE, 28, 36
Dissertation Abstracts International,
122
Education Index, 46-48
ERIC, 28-46
Historical Abstracts, 1775-1945, 62
Psychological Abstracts, 48-52

RIE, 28, 29-36
Sociological Abstracts, 53-54
Sociology of Education Abstracts, 54
Inquiry
    historical, 5
    philosophical, 3-5
Institution Index (RIE), 34
Instructional strategies, 83-84
Interaction analysis, 67
Interviews, footnote and bibliographic
    forms for, 124

Jacobson, Lenore, 66
Journal articles, footnote and biblio-
    graphic forms for, 119

Kalvelage, Carl, 105

Law of Effect, 72-73
Law of Exercise, Thorndike's, 72-73
Lesson plans, 81
Libraries, use of, 23-58
    bibliography, preparation of, 58
    *Child Development Abstracts and
        Bibliography*, 52-53
    Dewey decimal classification, 24-25
    ERIC (Educational Resources Infor-
        mation Center), 28-46
        CIJE (Current Index to Journals
            in Education), 36-46
        RIE (Research in Education),
            29-36
    Library of Congress classification,
        23, 25-28
    Mental Measurement Yearbooks
        (Buros), 55-58
    Psychological Abstracts, 48-52
    Sociological Abstracts, 53-54
    Sociology of Education Abstracts, 54
Library of Congress classification, 23,
    25-28
Literature searches, 16-20
    in papers, 89
Longitudinal studies, 69-70

Magazine articles, footnote and biblio-
    graphic forms for, 120
Mastery learning papers, 76-77
Measurement. *See also* Tests and testing
    evaluation and, 77-79
    Mental Measurement Yearbooks,
        55-58
    questionnaires, surveys, and attitude
        scales, 68

of success in reaching goals, 84
    testing and, 9
Meetings, footnote and bibliographic
    forms for, 123-124
Mental Measurement Yearbooks (Buros),
    55-58
Methodology in papers, 111-112
Methods. *See* Curriculum and methods
Michael, William B., 76, 78
Microfiche, 29
Mimeographed reports, footnote and
    bibliographic forms for, 123
Monographs, footnote and bibliographic
    forms for, 120-121

National Technical Information Service
    (NTIS), footnote and biblio-
    graphic forms for, 122-123
New Thesaurus Terms (RIE), 36
Newspaper articles, footnote and biblio-
    graphic forms for, 120
NTIS. *See* National Technical Informa-
    tion Service

Operant conditioning experiments, 73-
    74
Organizing evidence, 21-22

Papers
    contents of, 87-90
    documentation in, 105-125
    form of, 96-104
    in specific fields, 59-84
    titles for, 21-22, 87-88
    topic selection, 15-22, 88
        limiting topic, 20-21
    writing behavioral objectives in, 76
    writing, of, 91-95
Paragraphs, 92
Philosophy of education, 3-5
    papers in, 60-61
Piaget, Jean, 4, 7, 70-71
Prekindergarten education, 4
Psychological Abstracts, 48-52
*Psychological Foundations of Learning
    and Teaching* (Wilson,
    Robeck, and Michael), 76, 78
Psychology
    developmental, 7, 69-71
    educational, 8-9, 72-77
Psychometry, 80
*Publication Manual of the American
    Psychological Association*,
    112-113

Pygmalion in the Classroom (Rosenthal and Jacobson), 66

Questionnaires, 68
Quintilian, 5, 16
Quotations, documentation of 107-109

Radio programs, footnote and biblio-
    graphic forms for, 124
Referents, indefinite, 94-95
*Research Guide for Undergraduates in
    Political Science* (Kalvelage,
    Segal, and Anderson), 105
Research Guide in History (Wilson), 61
Research in Education (RIE), 28, 29-36
Research papers. *See* Papers
RIE. *See* Research in Education
Robeck, Mildred C., 76, 78
Roget, Peter Mark, 94
Rosenthal, R., 66

Scales, attitude, 68
Secondary sources, 19-20
    footnote and bibliographic forms
        for, 118
Sentence structure, 93-94
*Seventh Mental Measurements Year-
    book, The* (Buros), 55-58, 79
Skinner, B. F., 4
Society for Research in Child Develop-
    ment, 52
Sociograms, 67
Sociological Abstracts, 53-54
Sociology of education, 6
    papers in, 64-67
Sociology of Education Abstracts, 54
Speeches, footnote and bibliographic
    forms for, 124
Subject index (RIE) 29-34
Surveys, 68

Tables in papers, 102-104
Tables of contents for papers, 96
Taxonomy of Educational Objectives
    (Bloom), 77-78
Television programs, footnote and
    bibliographic forms for, 124
Terman, L. M., 20
Tests and testing, 9. *See also* Evaluation;
    Measurement
    constructing, 77-78
    Mental Measurement Yearbooks, 55-
        58
    standardized, 78-79
Thesaurus of English Words and Phrases
    (Roget), 94
Thesaurus of ERIC Descriptors, 28, 29-
    34, 36, 43-46
Thorndike, E. L., 72-73
Thorndike, Robert L., 66
Thorndike's Law of Exercise, 72-73
Title pages for papers, 96
Titles for papers, 21-22, 87-88
Topics for papers, 15-22, 88
Torrance, E. P., 66
Trowbridge, M. H., 72-73
Typing of papers, 98
    headings in, 98-99
    illustrations and figures in, 99-102
    tables in, 102-104

White, Burton L., 7, 70
Wilson, John A. R., 76, 78
Wilson, John R. M., 61
Writing of papers, 91-95
    conciseness in, 91-92
    improving skills in, 92-95

Youth: The Years from Ten to Sixteen
    (Gesell), 71